Praise for *Always an Advocate*

Always an Advocate is a terrific book, and there have been very few as aptly named. Change requires a lot of effort. And when a righteous voice needs to be amplified, Angela rose to the challenge time and time again. Her seemingly endless supply of energy comes from her faith in God and her love of the underdog. She's been a fierce advocate for decades, a righteous voice. She positively impacted millions and I personally owe her a debt of gratitude. She's paved the way to a better life for me, my family and countless other~ ~~ you Angela!

~ BILL KLEIN
Co-author of *Life Is Short*
and Co-Star of TLC's *Little Couple*

I first had the pleasure of knowing Angela Muir \ ten, both personally and professionally, during our w(gether at the Coalition for Independent Living Options in South Florida. I knew her as a steadfast, energetic, and creative individual, dedicated to the mission of advocating for people with disabilities.

In *Always an Advocate*, her third book on dwarfism, she chronicles the politics and leadership challenges in the Little People of America (LPA) organization, then tackles the monstrous "sport" of dwarf tossing, and finally explores her advocacy for people with disabilities who must fight for equal access in so many areas such as education, transportation, voting, and housing.

People are people. There are stories of power struggles, ambition, relationships, cruelty, struggles, and victories. There are also specific challenges which little people face.

You will not read *Always an Advocate* without being inspired and encouraged by Angela's determination to take on all challenges, and eventually overcome and master them with an ample dose of faith and humor thrown in for good measure. I thoroughly enjoyed reading this book and I encourage others to do so, especially if you think an obstacle is too big to vanquish.

~ GENEVIEVE COUSMINER, Esquire
Former Director of the Coalition for
Independent Living Options, Inc.

Angela Muir Van Etten and her husband, Robert, have been respected members of the dwarfism community for many years. In her latest book, *Always an Advocate*, she tells the story of a turbulent era within LPA, recounts her campaign against the demeaning and dangerous practice of dwarf tossing, and writes about her work on public access issues for people with dwarfism and other disabilities. You will learn a lot about the challenges that dwarfs face in their everyday lives — and about the life and activism of this remarkable woman.

~ DAN KENNEDY
Author of *Little People: Learning to See the World Through My Daughter's Eyes*

As I considered running for president of LPA, I asked a former president about the time commitment. "Two to three hours a week," the former president told me. *Always an Advocate* taught me that two to three hours a week was just a fraction of time compared to the 25 hours a week that Angela Van Etten dedicated to little people during the time she and her husband served the organization. Perhaps if I had asked Van Etten about the time commitment, I would have shied away from running for office. But I am glad I didn't. As a former President of LPA, I am proud to be in the same company as Angela Van Etten. I am proud to be part of a community to which Van Etten contributed so much. *Always an Advocate* is a testament to Van Etten's dedication and commitment to service. Through this service, Van Etten contributed in countless ways to the advancement of the dwarfism community, the disability community, and the broader community.

~ Gary Arnold
Past President of Little People of America

Sovereign LORD,
you made the earth and the sky by your
great power and might;
nothing is too difficult for you.
~ Jeremiah 32:17 (GNT)

Robert
My friend and husband of 40 years who has always
stood with me when I am called
to seemingly impossible tasks
and given me his love, advice, help, and encouragement

In Memoriam
Tom Aquafredda
George Baehm
Billy Barty
The Bradford brothers: Randy, David, and Bill
Mary Carten
Tim Deatherage
Paul and Ellie Jones
David and Lori Kelly
Lee Kitchens
Oleksij (Alex) Krywonos
Ed and Pat Lang
Tricia Mason
Harry and Carol McDonald
Paul Steven Miller
Gerald Rasa
Robin Zeltner Snider
Al and Harriet Stickney
Jim Tatman

Table of Contents

Table of Abbreviations

ABA	American Bankers Association
Access Board	Architectural and Transportation Barriers Compliance Board
ADA	Americans with Disabilities Act of 1990
ADAAG	Americans with Disabilities Act Accessibility Guidelines
ADAPT	American Disabled for Accessible Public Transit
ALJ	Administrative Law Judge
ANSI	American National Standards Institute
ANSI Access Committee	ICC/ANSI A117.1 Committee on Accessible and Usable Buildings and Facilities
ARC	Advocates for the Rights of the Challenged
ARRG	Association for Research into Restricted Growth
ASL	American Sign Language
BIP	Behavior intervention plan
BOCC	Board of county commissioners
BOMA	Building Owners and Manufacturer's Association
CIL	Center for independent living
CILO	Coalition for Independent Living Options, Inc.
CTC	Community transportation coordinator
CTD	Commission for the Transportation Disadvantaged
D	Democrat
DAAA	Dwarf Athletic Association of America

DBPR	Department of Business and Professional Regulation
DHHS	Deaf and Hard of Hearing Services
EBD	Emotional and behavioral disorder
EPD	Emergency Preparedness for People with Disabilities
ESE	Exceptional Student Education
EViD	Electronic voting identification
FAIR	Fairness and Accuracy in Reporting
FILC	Florida Independent Living Council
FSIQ	Full-scale intelligence quotient
FY	Fiscal year
gas pump	Fuel-dispensing machine
GPMA	Gas Pump Manufacturers Association
HB	House bill
HOA	Homeowner association
IBC	International Building Code
ICC/ANSI	International Code Council / American National Standards Institute
ICU	Intensive care unit
IDEA	Individual with Disabilities Education Act
IEP	Individual education plan
IRS	Internal Revenue Service
IT	Information technology
LCB	Local coordinating board
LP	Little person
LPA	Little People of America
LPNZ	Little People of New Zealand
MAB	Medical Advisory Board
Medwaiver	Medicaid Waiver
MIND	Martin Interagency Network on Disabilities

MRF	Membership Renewal Form
NEII	National Elevator Industry Institute
NOAA	National Oceanic and Atmospheric Administration
R	Republican
RE	Raiser's Edge
RTI	Response to intervention
S	Senate
SGA	Substantial gainful activity
SOUL	Supporting Overcoming Understanding Loving
SSA	Social Security Administration
SSI	Supplemental Security Income
TD LCB	Transportation Disadvantaged Local Coordinating Board
TDSP	Transportation Disadvantaged Service Plan
UPI	United Press International

Foreword

What is an advocate? Some define it as a person who represents another's interest. After reading *Always an Advocate*, you will learn that advocacy means more than appearing in a court of law. In fact, advocacy can be exercised in many different ways.

Angela has been admitted to practice law in New Zealand, Ohio, and New York. She has advocated for clients in civil and criminal courts. However, she has also advocated in the court of public opinion and won. For example, she and her husband, Robert, initiated and supported disability coalitions to protest the rise of dwarf tossing in several US states. This effort was successful, but in Florida she and others had to remobilize and defeat a potential resurgence of the practice in later years. In addition to newspaper articles, and media interviews, Angela met with state legislators to assure that the Florida law would not be amended to permit dwarf tossing.

You will delight and be impressed with her experiences as a volunteer advocate. Over the years, Angela has the distinction of being a Saul Alinsky trainee dropout, picketed for accessible public transit, and fought with Yellow Cab to obtain a ride in an accessible taxi that would transport both herself and her scooter. She was almost arrested at the St. Louis Zoo when she and her husband were denied permission to board the zoo-line railroad with their wheelchair. And the seven-year battle to lower the reach range by six inches in public buildings and facilities is documented in detail. This historic change allows thousands of people with disabilities and individuals with short stature to independently use ATMs, gas pumps, elevators, and so much more.

To the list we could add Angela's employment as an advocacy specialist where she represented clients in Social Security cases; sat on a task force to provide emergency services for people with disabilities; assured that voting equipment was accessible; met with Homeowner Association (HOA) board members and staff to resist HOA rules that denied reasonable accommodation to their residents with disabilities; served as a member of a local Transportation Disadvantaged Coordinating Board, and so much more.

This book offers the reader a grand tour of local, State, and Federal opportunities for advocacy with or without a law degree. The only requirement for advocacy—as Angela recounts—is passion, dedication, a thick skin, patience, and a sense of humor.

~ JIM KAY
LPA Historian

Preface

A high school student recently asked me a question following my disability sensitivity presentation. It wasn't the typical question a person with dwarfism gets—about clothes, driving, the height of my siblings, or if I have children.

No, the question was, "How long have you been an advocate?"

I had to think about that one for a moment; then it dawned on me. I have been an advocate for as long as I can remember. Always.

Always an Advocate, the third book in my dwarfism trilogy, is organized into three parts without being tied to a timeline. The focus of part 1 is Little People of America (LPA), emphasizing the leadership challenges in a volunteer organization. Dwarf tossing warranted its own division (part 2) given the recurring nature of the atrocity from 1985 to 2011. In order to provide a complete picture, chapters 8-10 are an edited version of the last chapter in my first book, *Dwarfs Don't Live in Doll Houses.* Part 3 on equal access covers issues related to transportation, access to the built environment, and my work advocating for people with disabilities as it relates to education, emergency operations, housing, social security benefits, transit funding, and voting.

Liberal use of pseudonyms—identified with a first name in italics—protects individual privacy and avoids publicly disparaging those whose negative behaviors were harmful. Actual names are used when permission was granted and to recognize the contribution of those who advocated for positive changes.

My prayer is that this book shows that advocacy makes change possible when people are willing to call out what is wrong, care enough to stand up for what is right, commit to the cause for as long as it takes, choose the right forum, collaborate and form coalitions with like-minded people and organizations, communicate with honesty and respect, and have confidence in God's ability to change hearts and minds.

Be an advocate for positive change. Don't hold back because of the size of the task. Advocacy success is not measured by outcomes or how we compare with others. Rather, it is measured by how we use our God-given talents. We only fail when we squander our abilities and live to please ourselves. I pray that people will pick up the advocacy baton, not imitating me, but rather relying on God, the Source of my determination and understanding of what is right and just.

PART I

Volunteer
Leadership
Challenges

Chapter 1

International Union of Presidents

Meeting in Washington, DC

Our lives were about to change forever. By all appearances it was just another day in the life of two presidents when we met at the New Zealand Embassy in March 1981. As president of Little People of America (LPA), Bobby Van Etten represented a nonprofit organization that provides support and information to people of short stature and their families. As president of Little People of New Zealand (LPNZ) and a Winston Churchill fellow, I was there to further my research of American disability civil rights laws and public relations programs.

We had no idea our business meeting would blossom into romance and marriage seven months later.

Inhouse Assistant

After 16 months of going it alone as LPA president, Bobby acquired an in-house assistant when he married me in October 1981. Aside from all the other benefits of marriage, he gained a partner with whom to share the workload. I was both willing and able to pitch in. After all, I had time on my hands while waiting to start law school in the fall of 1982. And he sure needed the help. His presidential load was ten times what I had carried in New Zealand—literally, since LPA membership numbered about 3,000 compared to LPNZ's membership of about 300.

Well before the invention of the Internet, communication was limited to phone calls and snail mail. Thus, Bobby spent most of his spare time on the phone, writing letters, and preparing the *Golden Sheet*—a monthly bulletin mailed to about 80 elected and appointed LPA officers throughout the country. The *Golden Sheet* covered routine administrative matters plus personal updates such as the medical status of an officer in the hospital. Individual letters handled more sticky situations, such as people not following through on their commitments or failing to work well together. For example, in 1982, correspondence was necessary to resolve a dispute among LPA founding members about the historic record being prepared for publication in the souvenir book marking 25 years since the founding of LPA by actor and advocate Billy Barty.

Media interviews and public speaking were also among Bobby's presidential duties. On January 28, 1982, we got a kick out of the limousine ride to a television studio for an interview about LPA on *Good Morning Washington* with John Corchran. As the guest speaker at a Tall Club International meeting, Bobby took pleasure in drawing parallels between people of short and tall stature.

At the end of Bobby's day at the office and LPA work at night, there was rarely a moment to just relax. So, I did everything I could to lessen his load and free up some couple time. Bobby saw me as a willing resource who could benefit LPA. This worked out well for us until Bobby gave me credit for my work. Bobby had broken LPA's silent rule that the husband take credit for his wife's contribution and he was criticized for being too reliant on my opinions.

First International Conference for Little People

As LPA president, Bobby was an ex officio member of the committee planning the first International Conference for Little People held in Washington, DC, from April 21-30, 1982. Although not an official member of the planning committee, I attended many meetings with Bobby and was able to contribute my perspective as a resident alien from New Zealand.

The conference goal of improving the quality of life for little people throughout the world was advanced when 80 delegates representing eight countries attended. The conference program was comparable to a national LPA convention with a welcome reception, medical clinic, workshops, media, fashion and talent shows, and sight-seeing. International delegates met to share their country's LP activities, select a delegate to represent their country after the conference, and vote for an international coordinator to act as a central communication contact and clearinghouse.

Bobby and I both led workshops and participated in a press conference and radio interview. Bobby served as the medical liaison for the medical clinic and media. It hurt when my contribution wasn't acknowledged by some LPA conference committee members. I retreated to the bathroom in tears when one committee member ripped into me for not helping with registration even though the conference chairperson had asked me to work on something else at the same time. Bobby was furious when my nomination for LPA's international coordinator position was not accepted. And a glaring omission occurred when flowers were presented to all the women on the conference committee except me. It took a delegate from Sweden to recognize the faux pas and thank me for my contribution.

LPA's 25th anniversary

Reno, Nevada, was my first national convention in July 1982, on LPA's 25th anniversary. Everything seemed in order when we arrived at the Baltimore/Washington International Airport one hour before departure. Yet when we looked at the bags unloaded from the cab, there was one missing. As newly-weds not yet accustomed to traveling together, each of us assumed the other had loaded the missing bag into the cab—the critical bag with all the materials Bobby needed for the LPA Board meetings.

There was no time for discussion as Bobby attempted to beat the clock. Incredibly, he found the same cab driver to race him to the apartment and back to the airport. Our plane was at the closest gate, and airline staff rushed us to the plane in wheelchairs in time to be on the right side of the door when it closed.

Our accommodation for the convention week was in the Governor's Suite of Harrah's hotel. Total luxury. We had two bathrooms, two refrigerators, an icemaker, a furnished lounge, and a fully stocked bar in a corner room with a balcony, and windows giving views of both the sunrise and sunset. To cap it off, the room was complimentary as a fringe benefit of Bobby being LPA president. Although it didn't compensate for the seemingly endless volunteer hours, appreciation for a year's hard work was welcome.

Harrah's excelled in catering to little people. They installed wands at the elevators to reach the buttons. Carpeted steps were in elevators, at the registration desk, in bathrooms, and even at casino tables. But LPA meetings and the media consumed most of Bobby's time. Except for the presidential reception we hosted in our suite for LPA Board members, there was limited opportunity to take advantage of our room or the hotel amenities.

Bobby chose not to run for a second two-year term in July 1982, but he didn't end his presidency without a stir. There were two presidential candidates for the 1982-1984 term and Bobby's tie-breaking vote decided the outcome of the election. Controversy also swirled around the election of the vice president. Bobby had to preside over the board meetings to resolve a bylaw dispute about whether one vice presidential candidate could run for a third term, and whether the other candidate was eligible to run due to a bounced membership check.

Ironically, even a good check wouldn't have settled my membership status. In 1982, a bylaw provision limited permanent LPA membership to US citizens. As an alien resident, I was only eligible for a foreign-affiliate membership if I had a job or was a student. Since I was neither employed nor a student yet, I was ineligible for membership. As a result, Bobby's home chapter—the South Florida Mini-Gators—proposed a bylaw amendment to allow permanent resident aliens to become LPA members. The bylaw passed with ten in favor and two against.

Again, without any effort on my part, I was in the spotlight as the coordinator of the LPA Fashion Show. Tradition called for the first lady to coordinate the show and so my service in this role was acceptable, albeit daunting. I had never seen, let alone coordinated, a fashion show at an LPA convention. Thankfully, I was able to reference a 1969 guide prepared by Mary Kitchens, a former first lady.

In keeping with the 25th anniversary theme, I prepared a commentary sharing some LPA historical trivia for the 650 conference attendees. In a break from tradition, I appointed two couples to host the show with their alternating commentary. However, I followed tradition in the closing segment of the show. In the grand finale, any couples married in the prior year could model their wedding clothes. Bobby and I were happy to oblige and used this time for some fun.

After being cooped up in the hotel most of the week, we valued our day trip to Virginia City, Nevada. This was *Bonanza* country and quite nostalgic for me—a childhood fan of the Cartwright family who had a crush on Hoss.

River rafting on the Truckee was more to Bobby's taste. Although, he would have preferred a river graded above novice standards with flat water, small waves, and only a few obstacles to maneuver around. Even so, his companions had enough excitement in the rapids and challenges running aground in shallow places. Most people would have no trouble jumping out of the raft and carrying it across the stones. But none of the four little people in our raft could do this easily. After one such incidence, Bobby tried to help Robin Zeltner, our last rafter struggling to climb back into the raft. When Robin couldn't get a grip to pull herself over the raft's edge, Bobby suggested she pass him her foot. If she had this level of dexterity, she wouldn't have needed help getting in the raft! But we couldn't give in to laughter until Robin was safely back in the raft. Somehow, we managed to pull her in and be on our way.

At the closing banquet ceremony, Bobby's work as president was recognized with a plaque for a job well done.

As past president he would continue as a board member for two more years, but we could now prioritize our own pursuits. Bobby planned to focus on his new job in medical research on dwarfism, and I would go to law school and take a bar exam to qualify as a lawyer in Maryland.

On our return flight to Baltimore, there was no

suitcase drama. Rather, we appreciated an upgrade from coach to first class. The flight attendant said they needed to redistribute the weight on the plane, and the other little people passengers didn't believe for a minute! *Who cared why?* Not us. We just savored the ride.

Incoming and outgoing LPA executive board members formally dressed for the convention banquet stand close together in a semi-circle looking at the camera. <u>From the left</u>—Robert Van Etten, unnamed, George Baehm, Lee Kitchens, Mary Carten, Lois Lamb, Ron Roskamp, and Daniel Margulies.

Chapter 2

President Robert: The Second Term

A Lot Can Happen in Two Years

After Bobby stepped down from the LPA presidency in July 1982 to focus on his marriage and career, we experienced a lot of changes:

- I started law school at the University of Maryland in August 1982.

- Bobby resigned from his medical research job in Baltimore in April 1983.

- We moved to Cleveland, Ohio, in June 1983.

- Bobby decided to use his given name, Robert.

- Robert began work as a Rehabilitation Engineer at Cleveland Metropolitan General Hospital in June 1983.

- I graduated from the University of Maryland School of Law with my juris doctor degree in December 1983.

- I took the Ohio bar exam in February and heard that I passed in May 1984.

Finishing What He Started

In 1984, Robert teamed up with his friend Paul Jones to seek a second term as LPA president with Paul running for vice president. I wasn't too pleased. Not only would it take us about 25 hours a week to stay on top of the volunteer workload, but I also didn't care for the stress that came with the LPA presidency. On top of that, I was in active job-search mode and didn't know how available I would be to help when I found a job. Plus, I preferred to continue writing my book, *Dwarfs Don't Live in Doll Houses*, which had already suffered significant delays since I started writing four years earlier.

Still, my preferences were overshadowed by Robert's desire to accomplish more for LPA than he did in his first term. Our courtship and marriage in 1981 had limited his ability to move LPA forward on his ambitious agenda items. As a result, I deferred to Robert's wishes to finish what he started in 1980.

Robert's highest priority was to broaden LPA's focus from being a nonprofit social organization to a 501(c)(3) tax-exempt organization. LPA was much more than a gathering of little people to make friends and find a spouse. It was also a great place to be educated on social, emotional, employment, environmental, medical, and other issues related to dwarfism. Robert believed it was time for LPA to seek IRS recognition of LPA's existing and future educational, medical, and charitable activities and thereby be eligible to receive tax-deductible donations.

Another driving agenda item was the need to give parents of children with dwarfism a voice in the organization. Sure, parents were a support group for one another—but in organizational matters, their opinions were not sought or even welcomed. Parents couldn't vote on decisions and were often relegated to the back of the room. In many chapters, parents were limited to servant roles of providing transportation to a meeting, setting up, and cleaning up after a meal.

Improved communications with the membership and chapters were also among his priorities. Robert envisioned a membership that was more informed and involved in decision-making.

LPA Conference in St. Louis

We drove the 500 miles from Cleveland, Ohio, to St. Louis, Missouri, for the LPA conference in July 1984. For the first part of the conference, Robert attended LPA Board meetings as past president. When he was declared the winner of the presidential election later in the week, he attended as president-elect. We were delighted that his running mate, Paul Jones, was elected as vice president. Robert and Paul looked forward to a productive term living in proximity to one another in Cleveland.

The reaction of two other friends attending a national LPA convention for the first time motivated me to support Robert's election as president:

Jay, the 17-year-old Robert and I chaperoned in St. Louis, said: "When I first arrived, I was very excited and nervous [. . .] The convention week was like being in a whole different world, like being normal."

Edna said, "I was fascinated by what I saw. It was like coming home, all the people your own size."

Tax Exemption for LPA

Robert's idea for LPA to seek tax-exempt status was energized at the 1983 national convention in Boston when talking with Martha Undercoffer, a paralegal from Cincinnati, Ohio. These informal discussions progressed to the formal appointment of the LPA Tax Exemption Committee[1] to explore the pros and cons of moving from a nonprofit social organization to a tax-exempt charitable and educational organization. In St. Louis, the committee reported to both the LPA Board and the general membership that a change in status wasn't only possible, but also necessary for the future growth of LPA programs and membership. LPA's path from an exclusively volunteer organization to paying for staff and professional services depended on it.

As expected with any significant change, there was resistance. But the Tax Exemption Committee was ready with informational flyers to answer those who said it could not and should not be done. LPA history was made when the members in St. Louis voted yes to amend the LPA charter and bylaws to align with IRS tax-exempt legal standards. Even so, the board postponed the filing of a tax-exempt application with the IRS until July 1985. Their intent was to give the districts a year to prove that they could meet the IRS financial reporting requirements.[2]

Presidential Duties

One of Robert's first duties in his second term as LPA president was to respond to a TV producer's request to name panelists to interview on the *Phil Donahue Show* in Chicago, Illinois, on August 8, 1984. Robert and I, a panel of eight,[3] and 16 LPA members in the audience[4] had the privilege of educating millions about little people and reaching out to potential new LPA members. Although Robert and I sat offstage, we still went through the green room experience with hair and make-up artists, a photo session with Phil, and had live microphones to facilitate joining in the panel discussion.

Less than one year into his second LPA presidential term, unexpected job changes caused Robert and I to move from

Phil Donahue Show LP panelists stand in two rows with Phil kneeling in the middle row and average-sized people stand in the back row. <u>Front row from the left</u>: Lenette Sawisch, Angela Van Etten, Mark Trombino, Brendan McDonald, and Robert Van Etten; <u>middle row from the left</u>: Leonard Sawisch (holding daughter Joelle), Phil Donahue (kneeling), and Harry McDonald; <u>back row from the left</u>: Charles I. Scott, Jr., MD, Betsy Trombino, and Carol McDonald.

Cleveland, Ohio, to Rochester, New York. This was disappointing since Robert and VP Paul Jones had valued a rare collaboration as national officers living within a half hour of each other. Even so, the collaboration continued from a distance.

As I anticipated, the LPA presidency demanded 20-25 volunteer hours per week and masterful skills to resolve disputes and deflect criticism, recruit and retain volunteers, coordinate meetings, propose policies, and continue communications. Some particularly thorny issues involved—

— publishing delays of the *LPA Today* magazine: three editors resigned due to hospitalization, getting married, and job changes.

— two travel agents vying for exclusive rights to promote travel services to the LPA conference in Puerto Vallarta.

— resignation of a committee member who spewed derisive and crude remarks about Robert and me after he received editorial input on a draft manual he wrote for LPA.

— district directors dispensing with LPA bylaws to meet separately from the national officers and proposing to elect their own chairperson.

In one of Robert's monthly *Golden Sheets* to the 80 or so national, district and chapter officers, he wrote:

> *I do not believe any member of LPA should be hauled over the coals for the views that they express, not even the president. Criticism is something most of us find easy to give. If we also remembered how hard it is to take, we might be more careful about how we expressed our differences.*

Such advice was necessary when volunteers resorted to name-calling and finger-pointing.

For example, one member called Robert a fool and said, "You have gone far and beyond your rightful place in corporate structure."

On a brighter note, one director took Robert's advice to heart and wrote a letter of apology with an agreement to dis-

agree. At the end of Robert's presidency in July 1986, a committee member wrote words of appreciation:

> *I want to tell you that you did a fantastic*
> *job and I really enjoyed working with you.*
> *The upcoming president will have a tough act*
> *to follow. Congratulations on a job well done.*

Symposiums and Conferences

Both Robert and I invested our time at Short Stature Sym-
posiums held in New Jersey,[5] Maryland,[6] and Michigan.[7] As
LPA president, Robert—with a foot in both the medical professional and patient worlds—welcomed both medical pro-
viders and little people. In 1979, he had benefited from multiple orthopedic surgeries, and now he was working in the
medical field as a rehabilitation engineer. He presented an
independent living workshop on modifications to provide
access to driving, the home and work site, and public places.
I contributed my expertise by leading workshops on legal
rights in employment and education and advocacy issues.

Puerto Vallarta, Mexico, was the location of LPA's annual conference in July 1985. The week was memorable—the
airlines lost our bags for two days (forcing Robert to
wear a borrowed women's blouse), we got dripping wet
from hot temperatures during the day and daily down-
pours at dinner time, and Robert and I took turns getting
Montezuma's revenge. Yet despite some discomfort, the
conference was a great success.

As is customary at a national conference, LPA reached
out to local little people through the media. This resulted in
several little people from Mexico attending the conference.
They were especially drawn to the traditional East versus
West softball game. Apparently, residents heard about the

game by word of mouth and filled the bleachers before the game ended. Language wasn't a barrier to anyone's enjoyment.

The Puerto Vallarta conference was the catalyst for the formation of an LP organization in Mexico. By 1988, Gente Pequeña en Mexico (Little People in Mexico) groups promoted Congreso Nacional (National Congress) November meetings in different states with activities akin to LPA.

In observing how kind and helpful the local residents were, one LPA member noticed that the people didn't stare as much. This fit Puerto Vallarta's reputation as "La ciudad más amigable del mundo" (the friendliest city in the world).

But residents repeatedly asked, "Do you know Hervé Villechaize?"

This wasn't surprising, given his fame from *Fantasy Island*—the TV show that aired from 1977-1984. Of course, most of us didn't know Hervé any better than the local residents, but his presence at the conference was hard to miss. Even though a little person at an LPA conference typically blends in with the crowd, Hervé stood out because two tall blonde scantily clad women who looked like supermodels went everywhere with him. His only interaction with members was agreeing to pose for photographs.

When we left the tourist cocoon of the beach-front hotel, we were confronted by the poverty of the local people who lived in substandard housing with roads in poor condition. The only way for me to reconcile the disparity was to consider the contribution of our tourist dollars to the economy which employed nearly 50% of the workforce. The alternative would have been to stay home and pretend such places didn't exist.

The highlight of Robert's week was parasailing off the beach. The highlight of my week was watching Robert land on the beach. The ground staff blew a whistle when it was time to pull the landing cord. I didn't think about Robert's hearing loss and inability to hear the whistle until after he was airborne. Thankfully, Robert had enough savvy to figure out his landing position without needing to hear the whistle.

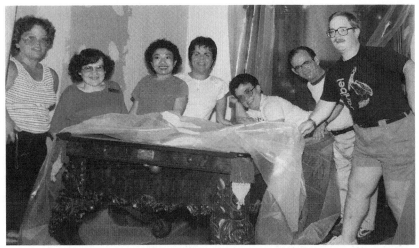

Group of little people flank three sides of Tom Thumb's pool table covered in a plastic sheet in an off-limits section of the Henry Ford Museum. <u>From the left</u>: Susan Conte Smith, Angela Van Etten, Linda McCulloh, MaryAnne Panarese, Helen Ford, Harold Ford, and Craig McCulloh.

At the July 1986 LPA conference in Dearborn, Michigan, Robert was glad to pass the gavel to the next president. Now he could relax and enjoy some of the local attractions. Having been to Greenfield Village and the Henry Ford Museum two years earlier, he had seen the exhibit of Tom Thumb's pool table and wanted to show it to a group of LP friends. But museum renovations made the table difficult to find. Robert finally found it in a restricted zone behind renovation curtains. Undeterred by the Do Not Enter signs, Robert led his party to uncover the heavy plastic sheeting protecting the pool table. I was grateful there were no pool cues in sight to tempt them to play on a table at the perfect height.

Mission Accomplished

Robert was satisfied with the accomplishments of his second term as president. In addition to keeping the LPA machinery in motion, he initiated or presided over several milestone events in LPA history:

- Charter and bylaw amendments that qualified LPA to apply for tax-exempt, section 501(c)(3) status with the IRS[8]

- A bylaw amendment giving the vote to one average-sized parent living in the household of a child with dwarfism

- The first mid-year meeting of the board

- The first annual LPA conference held outside the United States

- Discontinuation of the LPA royalty popularity contest

- Dissemination to districts and chapters of the District 2 Short Stature Library,[9] the forerunner to the LPA Medical Resource Center[10]

- The 1985 public relations campaign that led to the cancellation of a planned dwarf-tossing contest in Chicago[11]

- The foundation of the Dwarf Athletic Association of America (DAAA) in 1984, and incorporation of

six days of competition at the Dearborn National
LPA Conference in 1986.[12]

Chapter 3

Vision to Reshape LPA

Representing Florida and Puerto Rico

When Robert and I moved to Stuart, Florida, in 1998, we observed a leadership vacuum in LPA District 4, which represents Florida and Puerto Rico. We resisted pressure to run for any office, but from 1998 to 2000 agreed to share District 4 proxy duties in national LPA Board of Director meetings in Los Angeles, California; Portland, Oregon; and Minneapolis, Minnesota. It made sense because of our plans to attend each of these conferences to exhibit Adaptive Living's Ergo Chair in the LPA Expo. This brought us up to date on LPA national politics. What I didn't anticipate was Robert's interest in going beyond proxy duties.

In the fall of 2000, Robert ran for District 4 director and was elected to a three-year term on the board. In addition to national duties, he was responsible for organizing district regional meetings,[1] producing District 4 newsletters for a membership mailing list of 500, consulting with local chapters, coordinating media contacts, and generally encouraging members.

At the 2001 LPA national conference in Toronto, Canada—a city we had visited many times when living in Rochester, New York—Robert had a full agenda with board meetings, staffing the Adaptive Living Expo table, and conducting a workshop on adaptations in the home, school, or office. I presented a couple of workshops,[2] helped Robert at the Expo, and spent a good deal of my time in our hotel room working my telecommuting job. A bonus was seeing Corinne, a New Zealand delegate who had visited with us in Stuart before coming to the conference. We had also benefited from Corinne's gardening skills as she helped get my tropical garden under control.

Heights of Salt Lake City, Utah

Robert's second conference as District 4 director was in Salt Lake City, Utah, in July 2002 at the beginning of a new era in LPA history. Newly elected President *Noah* believed LPA had reached a plateau and was ready to take LPA to new heights, and had a vision to reshape LPA by focusing on six priorities:

(1) fundraising;
(2) local chapter membership;
(3) conferences and newsletters;
(4) technology infrastructure;
(5) the Medical Resource Center; and
(6) data analysis and statistics.

Robert and I compared the lofty goals to our climb up to the thrilling view at 11,000 feet from the "Roof of the Rockies" on the Snowbird Aerial Tram. The quick change in altitude made us light-headed. Likewise, the view of LPA's future was exhilarating, but the fast pace being planned made us dizzy.

Aside from LPA politics and Adaptive Living business, we made sure to see the Great Salt Lake. To my surprise, Robert agreed to take a boat trip without a fishing pole since the lake is so salty it has no fish. We also recaptured the spirit of the Old West on the Heber Valley steam train[3] and took a trip down memory lane with the Swinson family.[4]

Dan Kennedy, interviewed us for his book, *Little People: Learning to See the World Through My Daughter's Eyes.*[5]

Sudden Death of LPA Icon

Noah was well into his stride as LPA president when the news of the sudden death of Lee Kitchens rocked the LPA world on May 12, 2003. Lee was vice president of membership at the time, but his influence in LPA dated back to 1960. His untimely passing left many reflecting on how this icon had touched their lives as a Christian, engineer, father, friend, ham radio operator, historian, humanitarian, mayor, media spokesperson, mentor, pilot, Texan, and volunteer.

No one could fill Lee's shoes, but many hands had to complete the tasks he had on his plate when he died. For example, Daniel Margulies was appointed vice president of membership to complete Lee's term in office; and David Bradford relocated to Lee's home in Lubbock, Texas, for two months to complete conference registrations and help organize LPA archives.

The Boston conference in July 2003 was notable for Lee's absence, but also for the beginning of problems for President *Noah*. A deranged conference delegate caused a hotel evacuation after falsely stating he had planted a bomb, some unruly members disgraced themselves with excessive drinking and vandalization of hotel property, a member was expelled after giving pea-shooters to children, the hotel changed management in the middle of the conference week causing significant service problems, and Senior VP *Emma* resigned.

Rollout of Noah's Vision for LPA

Despite this bumpy backdrop, President *Noah* remained focused on his vision. He launched a plan for the future and longevity of LPA, opened an LPA office in his hometown, hired a full-time development director, and invested in a new database and software package. *Noah* was bemused by Robert's opinion that the plan wasn't ready to fly.

Robert finished his term as District 4 Director in the fall of 2003. He felt woozy when he looked to LPA's future with *Noah* leading LPA across this major crossroad. *Noah* would have done well to take a lesson from Salt Lake City's pedestrian safety system at crosswalks where pedestrians take an orange flag from a street pole holder, cross the street holding the flag, and deposit the flag in a holder on the other side.[6] In this scenario, the road is safely crossed and no one gets hurt. Robert tried to protect the integrity of LPA's investments and the toes of those who weren't of like mind with *Noah*.

A Sad Day in LPA History

Fifteen years after the 1988 publication of my book, *Dwarfs Don't Live in Doll Houses*, I made good use of my time between jobs and began work on the sequel. By January 2004, the synopsis was written, and a publisher's proposal was almost complete. But a distress call from my friend Monica Pratt brought book preparation to a halt.

Monica was the first LPA full-time paid employee and for six-and-a-half years, her home office was in Lubbock, Texas. She wasn't upset that LPA had temporarily moved its main office to President *Noah's* location. Indeed, she and her husband Neil Pratt were excited about the prospect of relocating to this town in June 2004. Monica's concern was with the sudden change of plans.

Initially, President *Noah* gave Monica until March 1, 2004, to decide whether to relocate. Then March became the month she was told to report for work at the new LPA office. When Monica said this couldn't happen, *Noah* gave her two weeks' notice to be there by the end of January for four to six weeks. Again, she refused. Monica needed the personal care assistance of her husband Neil who was under a school district contract until the end of June. Monica was then told that if she didn't come to the new office as directed, her Lubbock job would be phased out.

After Monica's fruitless negotiation with *Noah*, she asked me to advocate on her behalf. On January 20, 2004, I agreed to email *Noah* and ask him to reconsider his decision. I argued for Monica's position to continue remotely in Lubbock until the board met in July 2004 to consider whether the LPA office relocation was more than just a one-year experiment. My email reiterated Monica's terms for an employment contract, and further stated: "LPA is about people, not programs, and should not be dumping a priceless proven asset in exchange for an experimental speculative program."

But *Noah* interpreted my advocacy as a challenge to his prerogative to govern and make decisions that he considered best for LPA. His corporate background and lack of nonprofit experience made it clear that he did not appreciate the value of the relationship Monica had developed with the thousands of members and volunteers LPA depended on to achieve its purpose.

Instead of my advocacy opening the door for discussion, it slammed the door shut. Within one day, Monica received notice of the LPA Executive Committee's decision to close the Lubbock office, terminate her employment, and offer a severance payment of $5,000 that was only on the table for one day. I wanted Monica to appeal the decision to the board, but Lee Kitchens had trained her to stay out of LPA politics. She didn't want to ask the board to choose between hired staff and elected leaders. As a result, before the board learned anything about the termination, Monica signed the severance agreement.

This injustice compelled me to write "A Sad Day in LPA History," a memorandum to the LPA Board on January 26, 2004. I saw the loss to LPA as immeasurable. Lee Kitchen's sudden death had already left a vacuum, now LPA had lost his trainee with her vast experience and membership knowledge. My purpose was to sound an alarm regarding this poorly executed, flawed decision and challenge the board to be more involved in decision-making, to ask more questions, and to be leaders, not just followers.

The responses to my memorandum verified that some who had agreed to Monica's termination did so without all the facts. These members committed to being more vigilant and Vice President *Sophia* said, "Maybe the train needs to slow down a bit."

Chapter 4

Galvanize the Group
and Heal the Breaches

Venturing Out on a Limb

Someone asked if I had an interest in running for an LPA national office. I did not. I could see that the best way to make change in LPA was for a change of faces in the July 2004 election, but I didn't see politics in my near future. I much preferred to return to my original plan of writing our marriage memoir.

David Bradford, the volunteer chair of the Information Technology (IT) Committee, said it well on March 3, 2004: "The people who actually accomplish things in this world are those who are brave enough to go out on a limb, and brave enough to stay out there while everyone else is trying to shake them off."

David ventured out on a limb when he told President *Noah* of his interest in running for VP of membership in the 2004 election. The shaking began immediately.

The LPA Board was told that the relationship between David and *Noah* created a hostile working environment in the LPA office. As a result, *Noah* cut his office hours to avoid being in the office at the same time as David. In order to get *Noah* to return, the Executive Committee relieved David of his IT duties and office privileges. So, David hung on tight and formally announced his candidacy for VP of membership. The limb-shaking only intensified when David's district director told him he was ineligible to run for national office.

The next day, attention shifted from the question of David's eligibility as a candidate to a crisis concerning *Brooke*, who held a staff position as development director. *Brooke* resigned, citing a loss of confidence in President *Noah*. Despite his apology and plea, *Brooke* refused to reconsider. She was even more resolute in her decision to resign when *Noah* threatened her with a lawsuit. *Brooke* denied allegations based on scurrilous gossip and described the situation as rivaling the best Shakespearean tragedy. The dispute ended in June 2004 when the Executive Committee entered a separation agreement with *Brooke* that included a severance payment.

Three days later, *Noah* asked me for a parliamentarian opinion[1] on two conflicting LPA bylaws affecting David's eligibility—in one section David was eligible; in the other section he was ineligible. *Which conflicting bylaw should we follow?* In a memorandum to the board, I recommended allowing David's candidacy to avoid penalizing a candidate for flawed, contradictory bylaws.

On March 26, 2004, the board voted to support *Noah*, rejected my parliamentarian opinion, and found David ineligible to run for office. *Noah* took this as a vote of confidence and announced his candidacy to run for a second term as president.

He confirmed the rough road of the past several weeks and quoted *Brad*, his newly appointed LPA parliamentarian, "Moving LPA forward is like accelerated limb-lengthening on a 46-year-old diastrophic."

Noah called for picking up the pieces, healing the wounds, learning from our mistakes, and moving on.

LPA National Office Candidate

After his disqualification as a candidate, David asked me to run for vice president of membership and promised his technical support for IT issues. Robert completely got my attention when he said I should run for president. I was reluctant to run for any office. It meant shelving any work on our marriage memoir for more than two years. Also, after six months of unemployment, I was finally in the running for two jobs. I couldn't imagine taking on the LPA presidency at the same time as starting a new job.

At the same time, I was aware that my three months advocating for Monica as a non-board member had failed. I could see the need for an elected officer who would temper passion with patience, value staff and volunteers, work cooperatively as a team member, and promote a fair and equitable process. David was brave enough to stay out on the limb while people tried to shake him off—*how could I do less?*

After much prayer and discussion with Robert, my dilemma about running for president was resolved when *Jacob* stepped forward as a presidential candidate. But I did put the book on hold and decided to run for VP of membership with David in the wings to provide the technical support I would need for the database. Although I had never been on the LPA Executive Committee, I had board experience as parliamentarian, a District 4 proxy, and an administrative assistant during Robert's two terms as president. I was qualified for the position and change was critical. I announced my candidacy on March 31, 2004, one day before the April 1st deadline.

Campaign Platform

Jacob and I recruited *Rachel* as a senior vice-presidential candidate who shared our campaign values of respect, integrity, accountability, and inclusiveness. Our motto was, "Vote for people who value people." We held campaign meetings in online chat sessions. Supporters distributed our flyers at spring regional meetings and David created a campaign website called lpa4people.org. The campaign took off as we posted our platforms, biographies, endorsements, and commentaries.

One commentary posted my response to a media interview with LPA President *Noah*. Many little people were upset about the article and my commentary analyzed the objectionable elements.

My greatest concern was *Noah's* sales pitch for a stool his business sold to hotels: "Hey, guys, don't make me go to Washington and legislate lower counters for every handicapped room."

This threat was in direct conflict with the official LPA position that access changes benefiting little people shouldn't harm people with other disabilities—lower counters for little people would deny access to people who used wheelchairs. If *Noah* acted on the threat, it could undo ten years of LPA advocacy work collaborating with disability members on the ANSI Access Committee to find solutions that meet the needs of people with various disabilities.

The lpa4people campaign was bewildered when *Noah* didn't post a campaign website. Rather he sent attack emails our way and recruited others to post his negative communications on various listservs. We exercised restraint and didn't reciprocate with flame emails.

Four weeks into our campaign, *Noah* announced his decision not to seek re-election. In his swansong, *Noah* posted a "For the Record" message on a listserv read by many LPA members. He gave a rosy review of the high and low points of his presidency. The paid and volunteer staff who lived through the experience described the article as revisionist history.

However, no one disputed the closing statement that "the one common thread amongst us is that we all truly care and are committed to LPA being a viable and strong organization for [. . .] generations of LP families in the future."

Vice President of Membership Elect

As vice president elect of membership, I was encouraged by an email from past president Gerald Rasa expressing his confidence that I could "galvanize the group, heal breaches . . ., and keep the membership on balance." He congratulated me for "unselfish dedication, thoughtful inquiries which apparently preserved the good of the greater majority, and my energies."

I had no idea just how much dedication and energy the position would demand.

In the two months before the July 2004 election, the email exchanges with the board and candidates shifted to transition issues related to budgeting, fundraising, staffing, and the LPA office location and lease. *Noah* sent a private email to President-elect *Jacob* and me with the stated purpose of helping us to avoid pitfalls. It included a heavy dose of advice on significant issues with the inference being that we didn't understand that LPA had changed.

I found the advice of past president Gerald more insightful. Gerald recommended defining, prioritizing, and resolving issues; including people in the process and praising them for their work; and conducting myself with humility. He saw LPA as being in a downhill tumble—free-falling fast—and was glad I was getting ready to catch the avalanche.

Chapter 5

Destructive Forces and Direct Hits

Attacks on Newly Elected Executive Committee

In July 2004, insurgents loyal to LPA past president *Noah's* regime conducted guerilla-like warfare on newly elected Executive Committee members—President *Jacob*, Senior Vice President *Rachel* and me as vice president of membership. The assault began within hours of *Noah* passing the gavel to *Jacob*.

One of the Executive Committee's first agenda items in the board meeting was to hire David as a contractor to resolve the many membership database problems. This did not go as planned. During the discussion, District Director *Blake* made serious allegations against David. The Executive Committee had no choice but to put the hiring decision on hold, suspend David from database access, and appoint an impartial panel[1] to investigate and report back within two weeks.

The second attack came after the investigation of a district election for alleged partisanship, harassment, and unauthorized use of a district membership list for a campaign mailing. With references like "vendetta" and "welcome to the wild, wild west show," it felt like an arbitration between the Hatfields and the McCoys.[2] The Executive Committee's dilemma was that (1) the one calling for the election investigation was past president *Noah* seeking to join the board as a district director, and (2) the one charged with the mailing list malfeasance was the new Executive Committee's choice for *LPA Today* editor.

On behalf of the Executive Committee, I reported to the board our finding that the district should handle and recommend its own election policy. We didn't concede that use of the mailing list was a policy violation; but said even if the error was a violation, it didn't disqualify the individual from serving as editor. Our findings didn't satisfy the complainants or remove mounting discontent with the Executive Committee.

Two days later, we welcomed good news when *Jacob* became the proud father of his first child. In a much-needed moment of levity, *Brad* said that the baby was already studying the bylaws in anticipation of a lifetime of service to LPA.

And a week later, the heat went out of the district election dispute with the announcement of the election results. *Noah* won a seat on the board as a district director. But to the Executive Committee, this felt like Republican George W. Bush winning the 2004 presidential election and his rival, Democrat John Kerry, joining his cabinet.

As a board member, *Noah* quickly went to work undermining the Executive Committee. For three weeks, he agitated LPA members about LPA's historic records and circulated a false report that the Executive Committee had no concern for preserving LPA archives. *Noah* brought it to a head when he formed the separate Dwarfism Historical Preservation Society.

I responded with a "Yesterday, Today, and Tomorrow" email from the Executive Committee to the board and society members. *Rachel* likened it to the life-changing memo in

Jerry Maguire. It reminded her why we volunteer for LPA. We called for an end to the tug-of-war and committed to both preserving our history and planning our future. We challenged the society's separation from LPA and warned against repeating past turbulence. *The result?* Momentum for a separate historical society fizzled and archive preservation continued as a program—not an organization.

Hurricane Turbulence

Three days later, I was sending emails to family and the LPA Board about another kind of turbulence. Within 24 hours Hurricane Frances—a Category 4 with winds from 131-155 mph—was forecast to hit Stuart, Florida, a place where Robert told me they don't get hurricanes. Three board members—ones prone to sending disparaging emails—replied, expressing their concern and prayers for our safety.

We sheltered at home with five guests[3] because our house is hardened for hurricanes with concrete block construction, shutters, and a roof and garage door that meet specifications. In preparation for losing power, we had extra food,[4] water, batteries, gas for the grill, and cash. We ran water in the tub and had the pool as a reservoir for flushing toilets and taking birdbaths in the sink. We did our part to prepare and trusted God for the rest:

Through the Lord's mercies we are not consumed,
Because His compassions fail not.
They are new every morning;
Great is Your faithfulness.
The Lord is my portion, says my soul,
therefore I hope in Him.
The Lord is good to those who wait for Him,
To the soul who seeks Him.

~ Lamentations 3:22-25, NKJV

Stuart took a direct hit from Hurricane Frances—our unwelcome guest for almost two days. We listened to the weather reports huddled around a small television Robert hooked up to his boat battery.[5] Exhaustion kept us from following meteorologist recommendations to take the dog for a walk during the four-hour eye of the storm at 1:00 a.m. on Sunday. Sleeping was a better option—besides, we don't have a dog.

We thanked God for bringing us safely through the storm and especially for weakening Frances to a Category 2 hurricane with winds from 96-110 miles per hour. We only had minor soffit damage and some downed trees, while older homes had major roof damage, as well as blown-out walls and windows. Trees and branches littered most streets and yards, and a daylight curfew was in effect. We couldn't get to work, had no phone service for five days, and no power or running water for a week. Without air conditioning, we dripped perspiration and sleep was scarce.

To our shock, Hurricane Frances was a dress rehearsal for Hurricane Jeanne two weeks later. My repeated pleas for Robert not to take down all the shutters were in vain. He was preparing for the chapter meeting planned for our house the following weekend and couldn't imagine that Hurricane Jeanne would take a sudden turn in our direction. But when I came home from work early with news of Jeanne's pending arrival, Robert and his cousin Jeremy Chafin had just removed the last shutter. I was perturbed that, once again, we had to call on church volunteers to spend another three hours reattaching the shutters.

Jeanne was another direct hit and a Category 3 hurricane with winds from 111-130 miles per hour. The fierce winds slamming into the house were louder than Frances and caused the six[6] sheltering with us to pause frequently to watch the sliding glass doors wave along their tracks. We had serious doubts about whether the house would hold up. But we trusted God's word:

My refuge and my fortress, my God; in whom I trust.
~ Psalm 91:2, NASB

In contrast to Hurricane Frances, our household was wide-awake during Hurricane Jeanne's eye. We all went outside to view the damage and wonder at the contrasting calm. Robert, Bill, and Brett swam in the pool to cool off.

From the left: Robert, Bill, and Brett grin and raise their arms above their heads as they dare to swim in the eye of Hurricane Jeanne.

The rest of us made sure they came inside when we needed to re-close the porch shutters. We praised God when we came through unscathed and the roof and porch screen remained intact.[7] We lost more soffit, a few more trees, and the water softener lid. A neighbor found a stray lid in his yard and Robert was happy when it fit our tank. We were among the 97% of county residents who lost power and, once again, we went several days without phone service, or running water.

It didn't take long for hurricane jokes to circulate:

- You understand what that "two-percent hurricane deductible" phrase really means.

- You stop what you're doing and clap and wave when you see a convoy of power trucks come down your street; you cry when they don't stop.

- Crickets can increase their volume to overcome the sound of 14 generators.

- We would be rich if we had a store that sold only ice, chainsaws, gas, and generators.

- The new state flag has a blue tarp with "SEND HELP" in red.

Investigation Results Reported and Rejected

The LPA Board also had collateral damage from Hurricanes Frances and Jeanne. It delayed the Executive Committee report to the board of the investigation panel's findings about David's alleged impropriety. This delay was on top of the nine weeks we had already waited for the report that we requested within two weeks.

Finally, on September 30, President *Jacob* advised the board that David was cleared of any wrongdoing.[8] After refusing to cooperate in the panel's investigation, *Noah* rejected this finding and stirred up the board with his version of events. The Executive Committee answered by declaring the case closed and gave notice that any further communications about the matter would result in forwarding a copy of all confidential communications on the investigation to

David to discuss with his attorney. As hoped, this ended the discussion.

LPA Business Resumes and Stumbles

President *Jacob* had worked hard on the LPA budget, but the hurricanes twice caused him to postpone scheduled board meetings. Finally, on October 3, the budget was approved when the three Florida board members could participate in the conference call.

Meanwhile another crisis was brewing that couldn't be blamed on any hurricane. Board members asked legitimate questions about the status of the post-conference issue of *LPA Today*, the most popular magazine issue of the year. Although the issue was behind schedule, the editor was confident he could meet the board's December 4 deadline for delivery to the printer. But software conflicts and a weeklong hospitalization caused the editor to miss the deadline. As a result, VP *Ryan* took charge of editing the magazine and enlisted *Noah's* help.

Another deadline loomed. The annual Membership Renewal Form (MRF) should have been in the mail before the Christmas mail rush in December. Although I had written the cover letter, David's two-month suspension had prevented any work on the database mail merge. I ran for VP of membership on the premise that David would be the brains running IT operations. I couldn't do the job without him and persuaded the Executive Committee to wait for the investigation results before looking for another IT chairperson. When David's name was cleared, the Executive Committee appointed David to a volunteer IT position.

Several directors protested David's appointment. The resentment towards him ran so deep that his service was impossible—one withdrew his offer to sublease office space to

LPA; another accused me of lying; and in violation of LPA bylaws, one tried to change the procedure for Executive Committee appointments to the IT committee. Three days later, David resigned rather than remain the focus of a controversy that was so detrimental to the board's work. After being spurned by LPA multiple times David went his own way and took his knowledge of the LPA database and server with him.

The destructive forces on the board now had the Executive Committee on the ropes. Director *Noah* took charge of *LPA Today*, former VP *Joseph* generated the MRF mail merge, and newly elected officers were under extreme pressure. A December "We have a problem, folks . . ." email from Director *William* was highly critical. Among many spurious observations, he wrongly assumed that we didn't want our elected positions and only used the election to voice our opposition to past events.

On February 13, 2009, David Bradford died in his sleep from an undiagnosed respiratory condition. He was only 45 years old. Albeit too late for David to appreciate, he was posthumously awarded the LPA Distinguished Service Award in July 2009. Finally, others recognized his tireless service, skill, dedication, and loyalty to LPA.

Chapter 6

Presidential Relay Team

Call to Step Aside

President *Jacob* received several dictatorial emails from *Noah*. In one particularly nasty message he wrote, "I think it might be time for you and Angela to step aside [. . .] You have a job and a baby. If you move quickly things won't get any uglier."

This was the straw that broke the camel's back for President *Jacob*. He called me to say he would resign. He didn't see how he could accomplish anything in the current climate. *Jacob* was a gentle soul and this LPA "contact sport" was more than his health, family, or job could tolerate.

On December 11, 2004, *Jacob* tendered his resignation to the board. Unlike *Jacob*, neither Robert nor I saw it as my time to step aside. It would take a lot more shaking to throw me off the limb.

A "New Day" in LPA Politics Lasts Two Weeks

The LPA presidential role was so rough in 2004-2006 that it took a relay team of four presidents to complete the term. After President *Jacob* resigned, Senior VP *Rachel* succeeded to the presidency. She was more than capable of fulfilling presidential duties and called for a "new day" in LPA politics. After chairing her first board teleconference, *Noah* described President *Rachel* as "the best kept secret in LPA."

Regretfully, it only took about two weeks for the infighting to rear its ugly head again. The cycle recurred when the Executive Committee nominated a candidate to fill the senior VP position vacated by President *Rachel*. Although a board majority approved the nomination, some members were so intent on getting their nominee appointed that they lobbied against the bylaws to stop the Executive Committee from voting. LPA parliamentarian *Brad* ruled that the bylaws allowed Executive Committee members to vote on all board business.

Even so, a private New Year's email exchange with *Noah* gave me hope he could disagree on issues without flaming emails. We even shared spiritually.

I wrote, "I should do more praying than emailing." And we agreed on a prayer, "With God's help may we have more character successes than failures in 2005."

Yet, within days *Noah* sent me a private email saying, "You're in trouble. Things are a mess . . ."

He gave me one week to rectify the "problem." The next day he revoked the threat and apologized.

I continued to work hard[1] for LPA. President *Rachel* and I bent over backwards to appreciate *Noah's* efforts in producing a fantastic *LPA Today* issue. Yet this did nothing to stop board criticism of the Executive Committee. One director spoke for several board members when he demanded a reply within three days for a 32-item list of expectations from the Executive Committee. We answered within a more reasonable time frame and countered by asking for status reports on assignments directors had undertaken. This tactic stopped any further unreasonable demands being made exclusively against the Executive Committee.

Turning Point

The January 2005 strategic planning meeting in Orlando, Florida, was a positive turning point for the board. Perhaps due to the absence of the three district directors most critical of the Executive Committee, our facilitator[2] gently guided the board back to basics and forward to the future. Prior to the meeting, she invested three months in stakeholder interviews, an online survey of 100 LPA leaders, and planning with the Executive Committee.

At the strategic planning meeting, board members shared how LPA was personally meaningful. The Strength Deployment Inventory helped us understand how we react when things are going well and when faced with opposition and conflict. In addition to developing a strategic plan,[3] we made progress in developing a team spirit.

Executive Committee Initiatives and Perseverance

By February 2005, the Executive Committee *Monthly Messages*[4] to LPA leaders earned *Noah's* approval—he described one message as "fabulous." I also collaborated with a few board members on 2005 bylaw amendments despite their past criticism of the Executive Committee. Alas, positive email exchanges were more the exception than the norm for those absent from the strategic planning meeting.

Hiring an executive director was an important priority for the entire board. And it was understood that this needed to be added to the Strategic Plan. Consequently, on April 3, 2005, the board unanimously approved appointment of a work group to add the executive director to the plan. But board unity was short-lived. Before the work group wrote the executive director goal for inclusion in the Strategic Plan, Director *William* convinced the board to put the cart before the horse and direct the work group to begin candidate interviews. As a result, on June 27, 2005, the board named *Alyssa* as the interim executive director before employment and budget details were in place. It took another six months planning to get *Alyssa* on the job.[5]

Disappointment wouldn't begin to describe the ongoing frustration with finding a volunteer to oversee LPA IT issues. After finally finding a qualified candidate to fill the position, he resigned six months later. His priorities needed to shift back to family issues after his mother's death, his own illness, and his son's hospitalization. It didn't help that he received no cooperation from those with knowledge of LPA's computer system.

On the heels of this resignation, God encouraged me not to give up. Director *Matthew* thanked me for the time and effort I was dedicating to LPA. There was a friendly exchange with Director *William* whose communications were typically critical. *Brad* announced his engagement.

In July 2005, *Natalie* agreed to volunteer as LPA's database consultant.[6] She had the necessary skills for managing computer programs needed for membership renewal and retention. Directors *Noah* and *Christopher* sent complimentary emails about my *LPA Today* article, "How My Life Would Be Different Without LPA." Indeed this article explains my motivation for persevering in LPA leadership. It reminded me how much I appreciate LPA and how much members benefit from this great organization.

2005 LPA National Conference in Orlando

From the outside looking in, the 2005 LPA conference in Orlando, Florida, was a huge success. It set an all-time attendance record of 2,010 registrants. President *Rachel* managed the board meetings well with skillful use of the gavel. Robert managed a great expo of dwarfism-related products, presented at two workshops, and loved the company of his sister and cousin for a couple of days.

LPA past presidents—Robert Van Etten and Gerald Rasa—rest their feet at the Adaptive Living Expo table. Robert sits on a scooter and Gerald sits on an Ergo Chair for Little People.

From an insider's perspective, the story was vastly different. Our conference experience started poorly when President *Rachel* told the Executive Committee that both she and Senior VP *Ashley* were resigning. *Rachel* was tired of smiling through the constant accusations and barrage of insults from disparaging board members. *Ashley* was expecting her first child and was concerned about the potential complications of a pregnancy in which both parents have achondroplasia.

Rachel's plan was to announce her resignation at the beginning of the week and *Ashley*'s at the end of the week. The Executive Committee believed this would throw two days of meetings into turmoil, so we convinced *Rachel* to hold both announcements until the end of the week. Nonetheless, the knowledge that we would begin our second year in office with two more vacancies on the Executive Committee hung over our heads all week.

Rachel spared us this anguish when she decided to complete her term. Multiple young women told her during the conference week that they looked up to her as a role model, motivating her to remain president. She continued for their sake and was committed to hiring LPA's first executive director.

After holding it together for four days of meetings and helping Robert with the expo, I was really looking forward to my one and only free day at the end of the conference. I planned to ride off on my scooter and meander around a nearby shopping village with no schedule to keep. But my plan washed out when Robert pulled my wheels out from under me, literally.

I had loaned him my scooter at the expo to demonstrate the lift for getting the 100-pound scooter in and out of a vehicle. But when I returned to get my scooter at the end of the day, I saw a woman riding off on a scooter that looked like mine—and it was mine. I couldn't believe my eyes or ears when Robert told me he sold my scooter—that wasn't for sale.

How could he do this to me? Dealing with difficult board members was hard enough and now my own husband ran right over the top of me. He didn't see the problem because he planned to buy me a new and better scooter when we got home. But I needed the scooter then and there. *Why didn't he wait until the end of the conference before allowing the buyer to take possession?*

Exhaustion and exasperation barely describe my level of distress at this inexplicable disconnect from my needs. Robert's sister and cousin sharing our room helped me hold my fury in check.

Chapter 7

President Angela: Last Leg of Relay

President Rachel Resigns

The e-meeting President *Rachel* chaired to fill the vacancy for senior vice president was flawless and the decision was unanimous. But it didn't take long for another board tempest to erupt. In my attempt to hold off a financial decision affecting the LPA Medical Resource Center until the imminent announcement of a new IT chairperson who would help organize the membership data, Director *Ava* blasted me for delaying the board's progress. *Noah* added that I was stifling discussion and energy and attributed this to my being from New Zealand. I replied with a heritage and values email:

> *In 1893, New Zealand was the first self-governing country in the world to grant the vote to all adult women. I therefore come from a rich heritage of debate and democracy [. . .] there are three books sitting next to my computer monitor: a Bible, a dictionary, and a copy of the US Constitution. Please never mistake a plea for civility as a call to stifle discussion or energy. However, I strongly believe that the First Amendment freedom of speech comes with responsibility and is not a license to disrespect or discredit people.*

Earlier in the day, parliamentarian *Brad* privately observed that Robert "knows how to enjoy life" so perhaps we should put him in charge of LPA Board agendas. He also advised me not to forget to take a lesson from Robert on occasion to help reduce my stress level. Actually, the lesson I should have taken from Robert came back at me on our 24th wedding anniversary. President *Rachel* emailed the Executive Committee and once again announced her plan to resign. Undoubtedly, I should have listened to Robert 18 months earlier and run for president in July 2004 as he recommended.

An email from *Noah* to the board was the straw that broke *Rachel*'s back:

> *I just read the monthly report and quite frankly I must ask, "Where is Rachel?" This is the third time she has put up excuses for not attending to LPA business. The president's messages lack vision and substance [. . .] I'm starting to think [she] took this role just to use the title for [her] other endeavors.*

Rachel was rightfully offended by the inference that she had used the LPA presidency to support her appointment by George W. Bush to the U.S. Access Board. Nothing could be further from the truth. The appointment process began more than a year earlier, and I had written *Rachel* a reference on August 21, 2004. This disrespectful distortion of the facts finished *Rachel* off. Enough was enough.

Transition Plan

The Executive Committee responded immediately with a transition plan for *Rachel*'s resignation. This was essential because Senior VP *Hannah* not only declined to step up to the presidency, but also planned to resign her position.

Once again, we asked President *Rachel* to hold her announcement until we had all our ducks in a row. When everything was lined up, the Executive Committee set the ball in motion:

- *Rachel* announced her resignation on November 6, effective immediately.

- *Hannah* announced her resignation on November 7, effective immediately.

- Acting President *Adrian* called a teleconference board meeting for November 13 when he announced the Executive Committee's nominations to fill the two vacancies—me to serve as president and *Natalie* to take my place as vice president of Membership.

Despite Robert's support for my becoming president, some on the board did not agree. There was debate about taking the decision to the membership, but *Adrian* squelched that idea when he declined to be both acting president and vice president of finance during the time it would take to hold a special election. As a result, on November 13, 2005, the board accepted nominations and voted to fill the vacancies. *Natalie* and I were both elected.

Last Leg of Relay

In the congratulatory emails I received, people expressed comfort and confidence in my ability to lead LPA as president. What they didn't know was that my strength and courage came from God. In pursuit of Solomon's wisdom, I added his words as part of my email signature paragraph. For example, in February 2006, my 220 outgoing emails closed with this quote:

> *Pleasant words are a honeycomb,*
> *Sweet to the soul and healing to the bones.*
> ~ Proverbs 16:24, NASB

In running the last leg of the presidential relay, I determined to finish the work the original Executive Committee began in 2004. The only major controversy involved an April 2006 board proposal to waive the bylaw on the deadline for candidate announcements.[1] I found it incredible that once again I had to write an email to the board on the negative effect of bylaw violations. However, this time the board saw that following the bylaws was necessary for LPA's order and stability.

In addition to chairing LPA Board meetings,[2] my time as president was primarily spent as it should be:

- encouraging LPA leaders and members
- supervising staff
- coordinating with the development director
- coordinating with the Medical Advisory Board on research studies
- ensuring completion of the 2004-2005 annual report
- writing proposed bylaws
- helping plan the national conference in Milwaukee, Wisconsin

The Milwaukee conference was a great success. Robert and I were comfortable in the complimentary presidential suite and enjoyed sharing it on different nights with an LPA member attending his first conference—and Robert's cousins, Mark, Bob, and Linda. Ironically, I almost missed out on recording my presence at the conference. I'm at the top and center of the official conference group photo rounding the corner on my scooter at least 20 feet from the assembled group.

As president, I was pleased and honored to send written invitations, host an appreciation reception for the national leaders, write speeches, and present the 2006 awards for Media[3] and the Kitchens Meritorious Service[4] at the closing banquet. I was humbled when Director *Logan* presented me with a silver bracelet on behalf of the LPA Board members.

In a private ceremony, I presented an unofficial memorial gavel to the other members of the 2004-2006 Presidential Relay Team. It was engraved with all our names—*Jacob, Rachel, Adrian*, and Angela. We served in a turbulent time and held to our expressed campaign values of respect, integrity, accountability, and inclusiveness. It took the whole team to "galvanize the group, heal the breaches, and keep the membership on balance." Robert not only took our commemorative photo, but for two years had listened to my venting, helped troubleshoot issues, and encouraged me to stay the course.

About 2,000 volunteer hours after deciding to run for national office in April 2004, I was delighted and relieved to pass the official LPA gavel to newly elected President *Madison* for the 2006-2008 term.

Appendix A

How My Life Would Be Different If There Were No LPA

**—Van Etten, C. Angela.
Vice President of Membership, *LPA Today*, 2005.**

- I would not have married a president.

- I would have had no local LP community to welcome me when I moved from New Zealand to Virginia to Maryland to Ohio to New York to Florida.

- I would not get so many emails.

- I would never have read so many great books about dwarfism.

- I would not have enjoyed so much hospitality from members opening their homes for chapter meetings.

- I would not have been on the advocacy teams that defeated dwarf tossing in Chicago, Florida, and New York.

- I would have missed learning how the media censors the facts to promote a point of view.

- I would not have been criticized on the radio by Rush Limbaugh and Howard Stern on the same day for suggesting that little people have a "cause."

- I would not have attended 20 national conferences in fifteen states and three countries.

- I would not have gone river rafting in the afternoon and modeled my wedding dress in the evening at the LPA Fashion Show.

- I would have gotten a lot more sleep.

- I would not have bought so many T-shirts.

- I would not have met so many movie celebrities.

- I would not have shared a room with strangers.

- I would not have chaperoned a 17-year-old at his first LPA conference.

- I would not have earned so many frequent flyer miles.

- I would not have met so many little people from all over the world.

- I would not "know" so many people without knowing their names.

- I would not have seen an LP toddler grow from jumping up and down on my waterbed to graduating from college with a bright future ahead of him.

- I would not be able to use an ATM or reach the credit card reader on the gas pump at my local gas station.

- I would have fewer friends.

- I would have a lot more spare time.

- I would not have spent so many weeks of my life in meetings.

- I would not have learned Robert's Rules of Order so well.

- I never would have read the LPA bylaws or cared enough to try and change them.

- I would not have laughed so much.

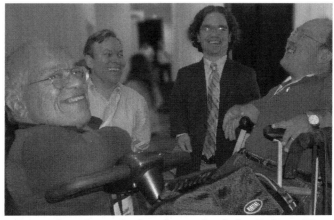

Grouped together in a circle—from the left—Robert Van Etten, Stephen Hatch, John Cressman, and Ron Piro share a good laugh at an LPA conference. Robert is seated in his scooter, Stephen and John are standing, and Ron is seated in his wheelchair.

- I would not have had my picture taken so many times.

- I would not have so many photo albums and collected so many newspaper articles about little people.

- I would never have stayed in so many hotels.

- I would have missed the free advice from medical experts in dwarfism.

- I would have missed meeting other little people with my diagnosis.

- I would not have attended so many workshops on topics related to dwarfism.

- I would not have talked to so many reporters.

- I would not have cried so much.

- I would not have encouraged so many parents to relax and raise their child with dwarfism with the same expectations and boundaries as their other children.

- I would never have used a scooter or wheelchair to extend my endurance and the long-term maintenance of my joints.

- I would not have learned the lessons that come from being in the majority.

- I would not have had to explain to so many people why the word "midget" is derogatory.

- I would not have been a guest in so many modified LP kitchens and seen how to modify my home for greater comfort and efficiency.

- I would have missed being in the melting pot of LP diagnoses, ethnicity, nationality, economic and cultural backgrounds.

- I would not have been helped with an LPA education scholarship.

- I would have missed all those chicken dinners.

- I would have missed learning the new Internet language, e.g. ;) and :) meaning wink and smile.

PART II

The Rise and Fall of Dwarf Tossing

Chapter 8

First Reports

Australian Nightclub Antics

In February 1985, I received a surprising call from a New York Daily News reporter. The surprise was in what the reporter said—not that she called me. She was responding to a United Press International (UPI) news release from Sydney, Australia, about the "sport" of dwarf tossing and the reporter figured I would have heard about it because I'm from New Zealand.

I didn't take the time to explain that New Zealand and Australia are two independent countries separated by 1,200 miles of ocean, and that what happens in Australia is not exactly local news in New Zealand. Rather my attention focused on the horror of what the reporter was saying. "Were the customers at the Penthouse Night Club in Surfers Paradise, Queensland, really being entertained by bouncers competing to see who could throw a dwarf the furthest?" As hard as it was to believe, that's exactly what she said.

The news was so disturbing, and the reporter so obviously ready for my critical comment, that I decided to break my rule of never making statements to the press over the telephone. This was a story that should not be printed without presenting the viewpoint of someone opposed to the depraved practice.

According to the UPI release, Robbie Randall, the Australian dwarf of four feet, considered the contest a fun thing and wasn't remotely worried about his safety. For protection, he wore a crash helmet and body padding and was thrown into a landing zone of mattresses. But the apparent consent of Randall and the precautions taken to prevent his injury did nothing to persuade me that dwarf tossing was okay, not even for those who enjoyed the excitement.

I denounced the practice as both degrading and dehumanizing and refused to label it as "sport." *How could it be a sport when a dwarf was the object of the competition rather than a part of it?* It sounded as absurd as replacing the javelin or shot put with a person. It definitely wasn't a sport for the dwarf being thrown. What's more, the dwarf couldn't accept any award for winning a contest. That would be as crazy as awarding a prize to the javelin or shot put, instead of the thrower.

Of course, once off the phone, I thought of many more reasons why this depraved practice wasn't a sport. I later read in newspaper accounts of dwarf tossing that I wasn't the only one to regard the practice of using a dwarf as a human missile to be a "spectacle which dehumanizes and degrades dwarfs to the point of being a mere object."[1] A Chicago Sun Times reporter questioned the game when he described it as an "alleged sport."[2]

For sure, there is nothing sporting about throwing a dwarf into the air, watching the person thump onto the ground, and then measuring how far he or she has flown. I decided the only way to be sporting about any of this nonsense was to do something to make sure this was the first and last to be heard of the practice. Surely, other people would agree that such competitions were not even fit for barroom or nightclub antics. I hoped that after this initial Australian fling, the dwarf would come to his senses, and the bouncers would return to tossing inanimate objects.

Royko Makes Light of the "Sport"

My disbelief and dismay at the news of dwarf tossing soon morphed into anger when I read the column of Mike Royko, a Chicago-based columnist and humorist. Royko not only reported on the Australian event, but actually questioned what all the fuss was about.[3] He professed to not understanding why some Australians saw the competition as an example of "man's inhumanity to little man."

After conceding that his view may amount to insensitivity, Royko further fanned my anger when he wondered if dwarf tossing might catch on in Chicago. He spoke to several Chicago tavern owners who went in for unusual forms of entertainment—like lip-syncing and ugly face contests—to see if they would host a dwarf-tossing contest. His column amused his readers with their responses:[4]

- A bar owner who regularly organized amateur non-talent Olympics approved dwarf tossing as a new event, because it was okay to juggle cats. So why not agree to throw dwarfs?

- Another owner appeared willing to host a competition for the benefit of abused dwarfs. However, his warped concern was revealed by his willingness to use a basketball hoop at one of his bars for "dwarf slam-dunking."

- A Greek tavern owner unwilling to sponsor an event jested: "Ees too dangerous. Maybe somebody get keeled—I don't mean the dwarf get keeled—what if dwarf heet a regular customer and keel him. How do I tell his wife what happen? And what do the wife tell her keeds? 'Hey keeds, I got bad news. Your daddy get keeled by a flying dwarf.'"

No Laughing Matter

Even though Royko concluded his column by saying that dwarf tossing in Chicago taverns wasn't such a great idea, he was amused by the prospect. In contrast, many little people who read his nationally syndicated column did not see dwarf tossing as anything to laugh about. Royko was soon to see this for himself. In a flood of letters and phone calls, Royko learned that little people are tired of being ridiculed and the butt of people's jokes, and object to being treated as a plaything of society.

The very idea of dwarf tossing smacks of high school pranks of a dwarf being stuffed upside down in a garbage can. It's tough teaching immature teenagers that it's no joke to have such short arms that you can't lift yourself out of the can. The idea of dwarf-tossing contests obviously shows that many of those teenagers carried their ignorance into adulthood.

The promotion of dwarf tossing as a "sport" convinced many little people not to tolerate being canned, dunked, or tossed. Craig McCulloh—the Pennsylvania Dutch LPA Chapter president from 1984-1986—demonstrated the intensity of many people's feelings when he wrote: "It's amazing how one's literary skills can be enhanced when rage and anger increases one's blood pressure beyond the boiling point."[5] Yet neither Craig, myself, nor other LPA members were satisfied to sit, bubble, and boil. We knew that our dignity and the public perception of little people were on the line. We knew that as advocates for ourselves and one another, we had to do something to preserve our dignity and to ensure that people would take us seriously.

Even in the 20th century, we found ourselves still working to dispel the public perception of little people as only being fit for the circus and "midget" wrestling. As one opponent of dwarf tossing wrote:

> *We are still seen as dwarf and "midget" caricatures, and fair game as objects for mirth and ridicule [. . .] Because of the images created by freak shows, the circus, and the* Snow White *genre of fairy tales, small people are still regarded as clowning stereotypes, alien, and somehow excluded from social acceptability.*[6]

The belief that society had progressed beyond those days was under attack. As a result, little people were unwilling to sit back and see years of progress fly out the window and plummet into a pile of padded mattresses.

Advocacy was the only hope for overcoming this assault. Indeed, as Robert Van Etten, the LPA national president from 1984-1986, espoused:

> *If we are to come anything close to ringside spectacles, it should be to fight for equality and justice. The prize really worth having is acceptance and self-respect.*[7]

LPA was fortunate to have Craig McCulloh emerge as the leader in the advocacy battle against dwarf tossing. Compelled to call Royko on the carpet for his actions, Craig wrote to Royko to express his outrage and deep concern over the insensitive, distasteful, offensive, and irresponsible column:

*It is one thing to report and inform peo-
ple of the news as it happens, ... However, for
you to attempt to describe and equate the incident as being humorous and for you to explore, hint or even suggest the possibility of
these particular contests taking place in this
country illustrates a sick mentality and dis-
plays total ignorance, the type of ignorance
and mentality which we in the Little People
of America, Inc., have fought against over the
past 25 years.*[8]

European Outcry

In the summer of 1985, LPA realized that the need for advocacy was not just a domestic issue. A letter from the organization representing little people in England and Wales—the
Association for Research into Restricted Growth (ARRG)—
informed LPA that dwarf tossing had spread to the United
Kingdom. Pam Rutt, the UK Action chairperson, also en-
closed a newspaper article which described the traveling
Throw the Dwarf show as being a great success in clubs and
pubs around the country.[9]

    The UK promoter promised that those selected as the
dwarf missile would avert any injury by training to fall in professional stuntman fashion by landing on mattresses, and by
only being thrown by the club's doorman. The restriction to
the doorman was to protect the dwarf from inebriated members of the audience who might get it into their heads to try
out as a thrower on the dwarf-tossing team. However, later
reports showed that the promoter opened the competition
up to volunteer throwers from a hard-drinking crowd. According to the *Wall Street Journal*, a postal clerk won a fall
1985 contest in Edenbridge, England.[10]

As if that wasn't bad enough, Pam went on to say that things were getting worse. She reported that the English dwarf-tossing promoter, Danny Bamford, had just returned from dwarf-tossing tours in Canada and Finland. Next, he planned a tour to US military bases in West Germany and Australia for the International Dwarf-Tossing Contest. The *Wall Street Journal* added that the promoter was also planning a contest in Italy.[11]

The English and Europeans, well aware of the power of advocacy, were quick to take action. ARRG had already issued a press release condemning the practice and reporting the international outrage of little people. The release included a statement from India that described dwarf tossing as "grossly uncivilized." In October 1985, the Netherlands' organization for little people[12] noted that the negative image being shaped by dwarf tossing went far beyond the boundaries of Australia and Great Britain and issued a statement to 17 countries known at that time to have organizations for people of short stature.[13] In this statement, the Netherlands called for solidarity in the protest against dwarf tossing.

In response to the protests in England and Europe, newspapers began reporting objections to dwarf tossing in a humane society:

> *Does a sickening accident have to take place before people realize that dwarf throwing belongs to the Coliseum in ancient Rome, not the supposed "caring" society of the twentieth century?*[14]

Not content with newspaper articles and letters to the editor, the European protesters were successful in gaining a resolution from the European Parliament condemning the practice.[15] Pam engaged in a radio debate with the English promoter and ignorant members of the public. She also pub-licized a phone-in protest campaign through a daily news-paper.

Although neither the protests nor the resolution of the European Parliament was successful in stopping the English promoter continuing with his plans for dwarf-tossing com-petitions, he did have difficulty finding venues.

Chapter 9

Chicago Contest Planned

Syndicated Columnist Sets Stage for Event

When LPA learned that a dwarf-tossing contest was scheduled in its own backyard, members were already primed to advocate against it. The first public word came in October 1985 from the nationally syndicated columnist, Mike Royko. His daring to publish a second dwarf-tossing column caused his reputation in LPA to parallel that of Randy Newman who in 1978 achieved notoriety with his so-called satirical song called "Short People." Newman had described short people as having grubby little fingers, dirty little minds, and no reason to live.

This second Royko column set the stage for an event in Chicago. Despite his prediction that the contest would never take place, his reporting of the time, place, and prizes for the planned contest aroused significant interest. On the day of the event, the Chicago West Side bar hosting the contest was jam-packed with fans hoping to see a dwarf-tossing competition.[1]

Royko exacerbated the danger when he suggested a way to throw a dwarf even further.[2] He noted that the distance a dwarf is thrown is limited by rules calling for the dwarf to wear a harness which the tosser uses to make an underhanded throw. Royko observed that had the thrower been able to hold the dwarf by the ankles and spin a few times before releasing him, the dwarf would probably have been thrown into the next tavern. *What if somebody accepted Royko's new rule?* It's hard to imagine that a dwarf could live through that version of the game and bounce back to bow before a cheering crowd. Besides, as Royko added:

> *Yeah, it's probably not a good idea after all. It would be just a matter of time before somebody wanted to play catch.*[3]

When the Chicago bar scheduled the dwarf-tossing competition, Royko's curiosity could have been satisfied. He had discovered that there are Americans who pride themselves in advanced technology and enlightened thinking who are also willing to reduce themselves to uncivilized behavior and freak entertainment. However, Royko wasn't satisfied. He now wanted to know if those opposing such spectacles had the power to end it.

Royko's column[4] describing the protests in Australia and England and his projection that the contest would never take place in Chicago, rang more like a challenge to those opposing the event. *Did we have enough influence to get dwarf tossing stopped?* I imagine Royko was delighted at the emphatic responses to his two columns. With his first column, he aroused the interest of those eager to participate in dwarf tossing; in the second, he aroused the ire of those ready to stop it. To him the real sport was not to observe the specter of dwarf tossing itself, but to see which group in society would win out.

Well, whatever Royko's game was, he turned out not to be the only player. After November 4, 1985, media attention to the dwarf-tossing issue did not just wear the Royko label. He lost his front runner position when the *Wall Street Journal* ran a front-page article reporting the loud European "Outcry Over the Sport Called Dwarf Tossing."[5] Royko's personal opinion on the subject of dwarf tossing was now irrelevant. An event in Chicago had been scheduled for November and it was time for LPA to do something to stop it.

Campaign to Halt the Chicago Contest

Robert Van Etten launched LPA's campaign to protest the dwarf-tossing event. Steve Bratman, a CBS reporter, interviewed Robert for a 30-second radio spot he was preparing for syndication to CBS radio stations around the country. And LPA was delighted to discover the support of columnist Irv Kupcinet of the *Chicago Sun Times*—the competitor to Royko's paper. Kup, as he is called in Chicago, wrote in a November 1985 column:

> ... *a ridiculous "sport" called dwarf throwing ... is coming to Chicago ... the owner of a Public House is planning to introduce the demeaning endeavor on Sunday ... We've had two calls from two dwarfs associated with the Little People of America, 3-foot-4 Robert Van Etten of Rochester, N.Y., and 4-foot-10 Craig McCulloh of Harrisburg, Pa., both employed in normal jobs.*
>
> *THE TWO LEADERS of the Little People of America are justifiably incensed over the alleged sport and will seek means to halt the game as an appalling form of exploitation. Unfortunately, the participating dwarfs do so willingly and are paid for sailing through the air ... We recommend a much more appropriate game on Sunday – watch the Bears throw the Dallas Cowboys for distance.*[6]

In addition, many individuals phoned and wrote to newspapers in protest. My letter to the editor of the *Wall Street Journal* was published on November 22, 1985.[7] Beth Loyless, LPA membership coordinator from 1984-1986, and a resident of the Chicago metro area served as LPA's spokesperson for local radio and television. Although this resulted in Beth becoming the target of snide remarks from announcers of the radio station advertising the contest, as Craig McCulloh put it:

> *She was being heard and the public was listening. She was delivering our shared message that this contest was dehumanizing and morally wrong.*[8]

As much as the media was useful to stir up the public support for our cause, the media coverage alone would not achieve the result we were looking for—cancellation of the contest.

Robert happily gave Craig the reins to coordinate LPA's advocacy effort. And Craig successfully located a number of Chicago-area organizations who agreed that dwarf tossing did not belong in their city. As an assistant to a Pennsylvania state representative, Craig understood the dynamics of gaining community support. He reached out to a variety of groups, including disability organizations who advocate for the rights of people with disabilities, the Irish Catholic community, politicians, and legal representatives dedicated to protecting the civil rights of citizens. The combined efforts of these community groups were instrumental in putting pressure on both the tavern owner planning the contest and on the political nerve centers in Chicago.

The Illinois Attorney General's Office responded to a Chicago parent's complaint filed on behalf of her child with dwarfism and assigned an attorney to the case from the Division of Disability Advocacy. Given the short time remaining before the scheduled contest, the attorney engaged in creative negotiations with the bar owner. When called into the Attorney General's Office, the bar owner was confronted with the report that many little people, their families, and respectable citizens of the Chicago community were appalled by the prospect of such an event occurring in their city. He cooperated and agreed to cancel the contest.

Chicago Mayor Harold Washington also came down hard on dwarf tossing in a press statement which declared the contest as "degrading and mean spirited,[9] a danger to its participants, and repugnant to everyone truly committed to eliminating prejudice against any group."[10]

In addition, the mayor's office slapped a temporary restraining order on the bar owner prohibiting him from holding the dwarf-tossing contest unless he obtained the city license required for public amusement events. The court order was issued on the Friday afternoon before the planned Sunday event, leaving the bar owner no time to apply for the necessary license.

The bar owner's plan to have a little fun and get publicity had backfired. All in all, having a dwarf-tossing contest had been a bad business decision.

As a result of the advocacy efforts of Robert, Craig and the Chicago groups he contacted, Beth Loyless, and other LPA Chicago members—it was a delight to read newspaper headlines: "Dwarf toss event canceled here"[11] and "Dwarf Toss Banned."[12] The January 1986 issue of Esquire description of dwarf tossing as a "1985 Dubious Achievement in Entertainment and Sports" was equally satisfying.

LPA President Robert Van Etten and Chicago Mayor Harold Washington dressed in business attire seated side-by-side and looking at each other with the City of Chicago seal hanging on the wall above their heads.

Chapter 10

Stop the Spread

Winning the Battle but Not the War

In celebrating the Chicago contest cancellation, Craig Mc-Culloh warned:

> *We have won the battle [. . .] However, I must caution that we have not won the war. We must continue to utilize the power of advocacy, as it can work, as long as human decency prevails.*[1]
>
> *Such immoral contests could and may very well occur in [. . .] Philadelphia, Pennsylvania; Rochester, New York; or Anytown, USA.*[2]

Craig's warnings proved to be prophetic. Members of three LPA chapters were soon faced with the prospect of dwarf-tossing competitions in their hometowns:

- The Liberty Chapter in Philadelphia was threatened with a "Dwarf Chucking Contest" in a local café.[3]

- The New York Finger Lakes Chapter in Rochester was disturbed to see an advertisement placed in the personal column of a local newspaper by a three-foot-five-inch dwarf looking for a

400-pound tossing agent able to throw the dwarf at least 100 yards.[4]

- The Mohawk Valley Chapter of Albany, New York—coming in under Craig's prediction of Anytown, USA—was subjected to derogatory remarks by a local radio station.[5]

Nixing the Planned Philadelphia Contest

In Philadelphia, the contest was being promoted by John DeBella, the DJ host of the *Morning Zoo* on WMMR, a local FM radio station. DeBella soon learned that Liberty Chapter members were unwilling to stand by and see any little person be chucked one single inch. The only throwing they would tolerate was that of their corporate weight against the DJ to get the contest canceled.

Harry McDonald—LPA District 2 director from 1983-1986—headed the advocacy response in Philadelphia. After the successful efforts in Chicago, Harry knew just what action to take. Within hours, he had the support of both the mayor's office and the Human Relations Commission. He also called on Craig McCulloh of Harrisburg, Pennsylvania, to mobilize a community protest. Craig, who now had the home state advantage, used the same strategies applied in Chicago—he gained the support of local organizations.[6]

While Craig gathered community support, Harry looked for media exposure. He knew the importance of turning the proposed contest into a public relations nightmare for the *Heart Throb Café* hosting the event. Harry contacted Terry Ruggles of WCAU-TV, a CBS affiliate. A couple of years earlier, Ruggles had conducted a positive interview about Harry and LPA's Liberty Chapter and invited Harry to call on his services anytime he had a good cause to promote. And

Ruggles was true to his word. Within a couple of hours of being contacted, Ruggles and a camera crew met with Harry to film for that night's five and eleven o'clock news programs.

While Harry and Craig worked on media and community support, other chapter members were busy getting newspaper coverage and making protest calls to both the radio station and the *Heart Throb Café*. One chapter member also contacted his congressman in Washington, DC. No stone was left unturned.

The United Cerebral Palsy (UCP) organization was responsible for turning over one of the most important stones. They contacted the owner of the building who was landlord to the *Heart Throb Café*. UCP was indignant that the owner would tolerate such degrading spectacles from one of its tenants. It was the right move. The owner was disturbed to hear of the planned contest and went to the café to investigate. *The result?* The *Heart Throb Café* owner demanded an on-air apology from DeBella himself.

Only one day after the promotion of the contest began, DeBella was on the air with an apology and announcement that the contest was cancelled. Victory within 24 hours! LPA's advocacy efforts won out once again.

Action in Upstate New York

The members of LPA's Mohawk Valley Chapter were faced with derisive remarks from WROW, a radio station in Albany, New York.[7] Even though the station was not actually promoting a contest, chapter members protested derogatory remarks before any proposal for a dwarf-tossing contest gained support.

LPA's New York Finger Lakes Chapter had an easier time dealing with the advertisement placed in the personal column of *Downtown: The Unbound Magazine* circulated in Rochester, New York. The ad's suggestion that a dwarf could be tossed 100 yards—when the unofficial record is only 30 feet —was absurd.[8]

As David Kelly, the president of the New York Finger Lakes Chapter from 1985-1987 quipped, "Even the best quarterback can't throw a dwarf that far!"

No doubt the April 1st publication revealed that the person placing the ad had a sense of humor as sick as DeBella in Philadelphia. In contrast, no community campaign was necessary. Negative reaction to the ad came from the DJ of a competing radio station. He had never heard of dwarf tossing and couldn't believe that such a thing would ever happen. Chapter members celebrated that the ad was ineffective in promoting dwarf tossing in Rochester. Human decency prevailed.

Why the Alleged Sport Should Be Outlawed

In all the United States cities in which the promotion of dwarf tossing had been proposed, the power of advocacy and creative negotiation were sufficient to get the contests canceled. *But what if Chicago's bar owner cared less about bad press and followed Royko's advice to obtain the appropriate license?*[9] *How would the Chicago mayor's office and LPA have stopped him then?*

There's no doubt that as powerful as public relations advocacy can be, it has limitations. Not all will be like the Chicago bar owner or the Philadelphia DJ who agreed to cancel a contest. Rather, some will be like the dwarf-tossing promoter in Britain who blatantly refused to give up his plans and reveled in the bad publicity.

> When negotiation and advocacy
> don't prompt a humane response,
> it will be necessary to make the
> offensive activity unlawful.

Legislation banning the practice may be the only way to stop the dehumanizing conduct. Even so, it's one thing to say a law is needed to get dwarf tossing stopped, but quite another to get it enacted.

In the case of dwarf tossing, a direct conflict between the rights of two groups of people is immediately apparent. President Robert posed the conflict to the elected and appointed LPA officials for resolution on November 4, 1985:

> *Should the desire of the individual dwarf who agrees to be thrown be overruled for the sake of the general dwarf population whose image suffers as a result? Does not the brutality and danger to the dwarf being thrown suggest we should take legal steps to have the sport outlawed?*

Indeed, those dwarfs being thrown regarded it as a job. According to Royko:

> *The Australian said it beat his regular job of acting in children's shows. He said he preferred flying across a barroom to performing before a horde of runny nosed kids. And the tiny Englishman, who is known as Lennie the Giant, said being tossed wasn't nearly as degrading as working on an assembly line.*[10]

The promoter who organized dwarf-tossing contests in England, said dwarf tossing, "allows the little fellow to show he can go out and be someone."[11] But if that was really the case, *why did the promoter advise "the little fellow" not to give his family name? What sort of recognition would Lennie the Giant ever receive if nobody ever got to know who he was?*

Of course, that's not to say it's the sort of recognition any self-respecting dwarf would be looking for, anyway. Just look at the audience who revel in this sort of spectacle. According to the *Wall Street Journal* account of the performance in a run-down section of a town south of London, Lennie the Giant seemed out of place in the seedy milieu where the audience was described as a hard-drinking crowd.[12]

Even if LPA members conceded that an individual dwarf has the right to make a living as a dwarf tossee, it is questionable just how good a living that would be. In England, Lennie was reported to be making only $72 a night, and he didn't have work every night.[13] *And what about the future?* The dwarf is totally subject to the changing whims of a bar-drinking crowd. In Australia, no more contests were planned in 1985 as, according to the manager of the bar holding the first competition—the novelty had worn off.[14]

Regardless of whether dwarf tossing is a viable employment option, many little people reject Royko's statement that a consenting adult dwarf who chooses to be tossed has such a right.[15] These contests fall into the category of freak-show entertainment. There is direct clash between the right of the dwarf tossee to earn a living as a freak, and the right of the nonparticipating dwarf population to earn a living in respectable occupations in which they aren't regarded as carnival acts or treated as subhuman objects.

At times, the State is called upon to decide that individual interests must bow to competing public interests. The State will act when it is necessary to protect public health, safety, and welfare. In my view, dwarf tossing is a case where the State must intervene to promote the interests of people in general, including little people. To do this, the State must elevate the right of its citizens to be protected above the right of the individual dwarf willing to be tossed.

Certainly, the State has a legitimate economic interest in fostering enlightened public understanding and attitudes towards the true nature and problems of little people. To permit Neolithic entertainment promotes the public view of little people as freaks. This perception makes it harder for little people to obtain the regular employment they are otherwise capable of engaging in. If nothing is done to change this concept, the State will be burdened with supporting many little people unable to find humane employment in the mainstream.[16]

Those promoting dwarf tossing claim it's okay because nobody gets hurt. The facts contradict such statements. The risk of physical damage to the thrown dwarf is not only high, but greater than it would be for an average-sized person. That's because most little people have potential or existing neurologic and orthopedic complications which affect the stability of their necks, spines, or joints. The stress of everyday living puts many little people at risk for surgery. Unquestionably, being thrown in a dwarf-tossing contest is an invitation to disaster. Even if the dwarf bounces back after the throw, there's no telling what long-term damage is done to the body. Every time a dwarf is used as a missile, he or she is preparing for a future in which there is a potential for dependence on wheels for mobility. There is a real possibility the dwarf will have no future at all.

I believe the State's interest in preserving life should

override the individual's freedom to risk his or her own life and safety. Stunt work and daredevil feats are common activities which have caused many states to enact laws prohibiting certain feats. Dwarf tossing most certainly falls into this category.

Any daredevil who lives through the experience of going over Niagara Falls in a barrel is met with both arrest and criminal penalties. Dwarfs who allow themselves to be tossed and those who do the tossing should also be penalized. This is one way of protecting the individual who consents to being thrown to his or her own injury or death.

Also, the danger isn't just limited to the dwarf being thrown in the bar. People with dwarfism objecting to the practice can't even dismiss the issue by saying: "If the dwarf being thrown is silly enough to take the chance, why should I worry about it?" People of short stature and their families have genuine concern that dwarf tossing will degenerate from the barroom toss of the consenting dwarf to the back alley toss of the nonconsenting dwarf.[17]

The fear of being attacked by thugs, drunks, and school bullies looking for fun and ignorant of both the social and physical consequences for the dwarf is very real. The upside-down trick in the garbage can truly looks like child's play by comparison. There's no way in the world dwarf tossing can be said to be okay because nobody gets hurt. Like Russian roulette, it's just a matter of time.

When Legislation is Necessary

Many view more legislation with trepidation and have little confidence in its ability to change public attitudes. I agree. You can't legislate away stigma. But where the majority of people believe discriminatory behavior is a breach of individual rights and should be made unlawful, then it is possible through legislation to protect the individual from the few who continue to discriminate. The stigma may remain, but its effect can be removed. For example, a promoter's support of dwarf tossing may continue, but the law will prevent his sponsoring any further events.

Yet in order for legislation to be effective, the majority must support it. Unless people agree that dwarf tossing is unacceptable entertainment in modern society, a law will never be enacted, enforcement efforts will be ineffectual, and the practice will continue unchecked.

Some have resisted the introduction of civil rights legislation on the premise that education is enough. However, it's naïve to believe that the opponents of various laws don't know what they're doing when they "forget" to put in the curb-cut, lower the elevator buttons, or promote the throwing of dwarfs. All the education in the world would never change the mind of someone like the British dwarf-tossing promoter. The Europeans surely did try.

Even if a person fails to recognize the rights of little people, the effect is no less adverse. It is irrelevant whether the action is deliberate or accidental. The fact remains, it's unequal treatment when the rights of little people are violated.

Nobody can deny there is already too much legislation and regulation, but this doesn't excuse refusal to pass legislation which is necessary to correct injustice. The answer is to re-evaluate existing legislation, prune what is redundant, and add what is needed for the protection of little people in society.

It's not a question of legislation or education. The two go hand-in-hand. To support legislation and not education ignores the problem of compliance. Laws are useless if people don't understand or want to obey them. The effect will be that people will do their best to circumvent the law. Likewise, to support education and not legislation presumes all people are tuned into the education program, and all will be convinced. This won't happen. Too many violations will fall between the cracks, and too many little people will suffer at the hands of discrimination.

> We need education and legislation working together to ensure understanding of the reason for the law, create support for it, and obtain compliance from those who would escape it if they could.

Even if the legislation is never used in enforcement proceedings, the threat of that expense is a deterrent in the mind of the person asked to comply with the law. Often a person will accede to a request to avoid costly and time-consuming legal proceedings. And, in the case of those who promote dwarf tossing, the law puts a tool in the hand of those ready to stop it long before it ever gets off the ground.

Chapter 11

Biting the Legislative Dust

Florida Law

In 1989, dwarf-tossing spectacles masqueraded as "sport" when barroom patrons in Florida competed for prize money awarded to whoever threw a dwarf the farthest or knocked down the most pins with a dwarf. A willing dwarf served as a human Frisbee when tossed into the air or as a bowling ball when strapped onto a skateboard.

I learned about this traveling road show when LPA advocates[1] in Florida called me at my New York residence. They had read the dwarf-tossing chapter in my 1988 book—*Dwarfs Don't Live in Doll Houses*—and quoted my observation:

> *When negotiation and advocacy don't prompt an appropriate response [. . .] legislation will be the only means to avert the action.*

The dwarf-tossing contests in Florida had thrived on negative publicity for a whole year. Any advocacy moves to shut down the contests failed because the promoters took the show on the road before local municipalities could prohibit the practice. Consequently, I agreed with the conclusion that a statewide law to make the offensive activity unlawful was needed. LPA advocates in Florida were successful in getting state lawmakers in both the house and senate to introduce a bill to ban dwarf tossing in licensed establishments.

My role in the passage of the Florida bill to ban dwarf tossing was minimal. However, on May 2, 1989, I was happy to help gain public support for the bill by joining Florida advocates as a guest on the *Sally Jessy Raphael Show*.[2] One of the points I made was that dwarf tossing affects all people with dwarfism because it endorses society's decision to strip dwarfs of their personhood and subject them to unequal treatment. For example, an employer may not take a job candidate with dwarfism seriously, wrongly believing that it's okay to discriminate because dwarfs are only good for freak show entertainment or objects of ridicule.

Dr. Cheryl Reid, a member of the LPA MAB, addressed the danger of dwarf tossing. She used an anatomical model to show that the spinal cord of dwarfs with achondroplasia— the most common type of dwarfism—has less room to move through the spinal column and is more likely to be kinked or bent.

Dr. Reid said, "If this occurs, it may cause sudden paralysis or death."

Support for her expert medical opinion came from quotes Sally read from other dwarfism doctors at nationally renowned medical centers.

Further medical evidence showed that there was no way to make dwarf tossing safe. For example, on April 27, 1989, Dr. Aldo F. Berti, Clinical Assistant Professor of Neurological Surgery at the University of Miami School of Medicine, wrote, "I do not believe any safety equipment used by the volunteer dwarves in their chosen risky business serves as significant protection since it does not give any stability to their weak musculoskeletal complexion."

Contrary to the predictions of Florida dwarf-tossing

promoters, the Florida bill became law on June 28, 1989.[3] According to Nancy Mayeux, the mother of two girls with dwarfism, the legislature found that dwarf tossing

(1) is morally wrong;

(2) creates discrimination against dwarfs;

(3) is a potential financial burden to the State when inevitable injury occurs to the uninsurable dwarf who is tossed;

(4) infringes on the rights of and endangers other dwarfs in the community; and

(5) is an embarrassment to the State.

Need for New York Law

Undaunted by the Florida legislative action, the dwarf-tossing promoters took their show to New York state. LPA was ready. At the national conference in July 1989, I accepted an appointment as the coordinator to get a similar law passed in the New York legislature.

Knowing the time commitment involved, Robert was reluctant for me to take this assignment and worried that it would be for naught if the law didn't pass. Yet I felt compelled to try and stop this despicable practice. I didn't need a guaranteed outcome and was ready to stand against such depravity. The sacrifice of my time was a small price to pay. Robert not only relented, but also sacrificed the special attention he deserved on his 40th birthday.

My first assignment was to build a coalition of people who shared my passion to stop dwarf tossing and dwarf bowling. In those pre-Internet days, it had to be done the old-fashioned way—with phone calls and snail mail. On July 17, 1989, I wrote the first of many letters to prospective members of the LPA New York Committee to Ban Dwarf Tossing.[4]

These letters invited people to join the campaign and gave updates on legislative activity, media reports, and finances. Each month, I spotlighted the exceptional work of an individual campaign volunteer. There was also guidance on writing to and visiting state legislators at critical steps in the bill's passage through the legislature. We greatly benefited from the legislative package prepared for the Florida campaign against dwarf tossing.[5]

Media on New York Bill

In addition to tracking media response to the New York bill, I did about 25 local, national, and international television, radio, and newspaper interviews. Although the coverage was mostly fair, in January 1990 I was on air with one radio shock-jock whose only intent was to ridicule little people.[6] He invited me to San Francisco where he offered to meet me at the airport, put me in his trunk, and take me to a place where he could throw me. His attitude was typical of the disrespect and derision dwarf tossing generated against people with dwarfism during this time.

In comparison, Phil Donahue hosted a show with a vigorous debate on the pros and cons of a ban on dwarf tossing and dwarf bowling in New York state-licensed establishments serving alcoholic beverages.[7] On October 12, 1989, Donahue opened his show on violent entertainment with the statement:

> *Well, they're throwing dwarfs—throwing live human beings. This looks like the most demeaning, humiliating, degrading, prejudice-provoking activity.*

Phil's guests included a medical researcher speaking

to the dangers of violent entertainment, the dwarf-tossing business owner and dwarf "tossee" who opposed the ban, and me lobbying for the ban. The majority of the audience appeared to favor the ban, but a sizeable group opposed infringing on the dwarf's freedom of choice to engage in dangerous activity. I responded with examples of the State making laws to protect individuals from the consequences of their own actions and to protect the State from the cost of injuries suffered by uninsured risk takers. I cited the example of laws fining people for going over Niagara Falls in a barrel and requiring people to wear seatbelts and motorcycle helmets.

After acknowledging the libertarian view, I challenged viewers, "Why is there an audience? [. . .] this is appealing to a lower instinct in people [. . .] The problem with dwarf tossing is that we're legitimizing bully behavior."

I thanked God for putting the words in my mouth on the *Phil Donahue Show*. The exposure helped propel the bill forward. Soon after the program, we had a draft of the New York bill.[8] As little people contacted their state representatives, legislators began signing on as bill co-sponsors. On December 21, 1989, it helped that Gary Abrams—a freelance writer for the Los Angeles Times—spurned dwarf tossing as the worst "sport" of the decade.

A few years later, more media attention made me a target of two polar opposite radio personalities—Howard Stern and Rush Limbaugh. Their comments showed the ignorance that leads society to think it's okay to make fun of people with dwarfism. In their radio talk shows both Stern and Limbaugh took umbrage with what I said to a *New York Post* reporter who had asked for my response to President Clinton's comment about Robert Reich, the Secretary of Labor.

When inspecting a three-foot-high Lego replica of the White House, the president joked that the four-foot-ten secretary "could almost live in there."[9]

After reading the *Post* article, Stern and Limbaugh were both steaming with my saying the joke was inappropriate—especially coming from the president—and didn't help our cause.

Limbaugh said, "What cause?"

As someone who never listens to either radio program, I didn't call in to answer the question. Thankfully, my friend, Robin Zeltner, called in to express indignation at their ignorance.

Support and Success for New York Law and Bar Exam

I couldn't imagine taking the New York State bar exam while working and coordinating the dwarf-tossing bill. But after studying the book of Joshua in my Bible study group, I claimed one of the promises God repeatedly made to Joshua in chapter 1—*Be strong and courageous*—and I registered to take the bar exam in July 1990. God gave me the strength to do both, along with the prayer support of the women in my study group.

Although the New York Senate bill passed in early July 1990, the Assembly bill almost died in both the Commerce and Codes committees. The Commerce Committee questioned the bill's constitutionality because of its interference with the right of a dwarf tossee to work; and the Codes Committee found the definition of dwarfism too vague. Carving out time to respond to these challenges was difficult.

I had a three-month plan: to work 40 hours a week and to study 25 hours a week for the bar exam. Frustration set in when I had to squeeze in time to write a five-page legal-opinion letter as to why the bill was constitutional. I also had to recruit two members of LPA's MAB—Dr. Cheryl Reid and Dr. Charles I. Scott, Jr.—to help Assembly committee staff draft text that precisely defined the people with dwarfism protected by the law.

But God supplied the stamina I needed to work, study, and advocate for the law. Finally, the constitutionality questions were resolved, the bill was reported out of both committees, and it passed in the Assembly on June 28, 1990. A conforming Senate bill passed on June 30, 1990.[10] The governor's signature was all that remained. Surely, he would agree that dwarf tossing and dwarf bowling were offensive by any standard of human decency.

Meanwhile, my study schedule caused me to depend on Robert for getting things done around the house. One duty involved supervising a couple of church youth working to raise money for a summer mission trip. We hired them to plant annuals in the flower garden. Robert gave them the plants, pointed them towards the garden, went back to his work, paid them when they announced completion, and let them leave without checking their work.

When I took a study break, I went outside ready to enjoy the fruit of their labor. I couldn't believe my eyes. I burst into tears when I saw the plants in the ground upside down. I watered the ground with tears as I dug out all the plants and replanted them with the roots in the ground and the green shoots facing the sun. Studying was supplanted by gardening.

Although Robert was stunned by the youths' ignorance, he didn't understand why I was so upset, and he made no effort to help me correct their mistake. No doubt, Robert was glad to get away from it all the following weekend when he went to his 20th high school reunion in Jupiter, Florida. He went

by himself because the reunion was the weekend before the
New York state bar exam.

July 24, 1990, was a great day—the first of two days of
the bar exam. Although I was more than ready to pour out
all I had learned onto paper, it wasn't the exam that made
the day great. No, it was great because of a call I received
from an AP reporter who told me that Governor Mario Cuomo had signed the New York bill to ban dwarf tossing in licensed establishments![11] I praised God as I went into day two
of the exam. And I'm sure Governor Cuomo appreciated a
reporter gracing him with a Humanitarian of the Year Award
for hanging tough against some strong criticism for signing
the bill into law.[12]

Relief and joy overflowed on September 20 and November 8, 1990, when I opened the mail reporting that I had
passed both the New York state bar and ethics exams. God
kept all His promises to me:

> *Not one word of all the good words*
> *which the LORD your God*
> *spoke concerning you has failed;*
> *all have been fulfilled for you,*
> *not one word of them has failed.*
> *~ Joshua 23:14, NASB*

Chapter 12

Give Me A Break

Radio Station Threatens Return

Despite being called one of the ten worst inventions of the millennium—alongside the Spanish Inquisition, advertising, and nuclear war[1]—dwarf tossing threatened to return to Florida during Robert's tenure as LPA District 4 director. In November 2001 Dave the Dwarf, a Tampa radio personality, filed a lawsuit asking a federal court not to enforce the 1989 Florida law that banned dwarf tossing in licensed establishments.

The lawsuit claimed that the law was unconstitutional and irrelevant to any valid public purpose. The plaintiff pleaded the right to start a dwarf-tossing business. The radio station used the litigation to launch a successful media stunt. And LPA in Florida resisted exploitive activity reminiscent of circus sideshows. As the LPA director for Florida, Robert appointed Nancy Mayeux—a mother of two children with dwarfism—as public relations director to manage the media onslaught that followed the lawsuit.[2]

The radio station was shrewd enough to pit LPA against Dave the Dwarf even though the named defendants in the lawsuit were the Florida governor and the Division of Alcoholic, Beverages and Tobacco. The station titillated its morning show audience by negatively portraying Dave as a piece of luggage to be tossed and LPA as a militant group interfering with his right to work.

Although the lawsuit was dismissed in February 2002, there was no hearing or ruling on the constitutionality of the law. Rather, the judge found he had no jurisdiction to hear the case because there were no agency rules to enforce the dwarf-tossing law. This was the first time LPA learned that the dwarf-tossing rules, in effect from 1989-1994, had been repealed as unnecessary.[3] As a result, the radio station began planning a dwarf-tossing event and LPA put pressure on the state of Florida to publish enforcement rules before the contest took place.

John Stossel Compromises Dwarfs

Meanwhile, John Stossel's "Give Me a Break" segment on ABC's *20/20* program aired on March 8, 2002. Robert and I had taped the show in December 2001 and naively believed that Stossel would fairly present both sides of the dwarf-tossing debate. He did not. Stossel's notoriety for unfair and inaccurate reports posing as journalism[4] had escaped my attention. After watching the *20/20* segment, I was so incensed that I sat up until the early hours of the morning writing a response called, "John Stossel Compromises Dwarfs in Name of Freedom."[5]

Despite our disgust with Stossel's biased report, many regarded our airtime as dignified, intelligent, rational, and well spoken. People encouraged us to keep fighting for the right thing and stand up for our beliefs. Barbara Walters— an acclaimed broadcast journalist—won the praise of many viewers when she nailed Stossel's libertarian view by comparing the dwarf-tossing law to society's ban on suicide, prostitution, and drug dealing.

Planned Event Canceled

Emboldened by the Stossel report and the judge's dismissal of the lawsuit, the Tampa radio station planned a dwarf-tossing event for April 5, 2002. The Florida Division of Alcoholic Beverages and Tobacco responded to my complaint about the planned event on LPA's behalf and issued a warning to the bar:

> *It is a violation of Florida* law [Florida Statute, Title XXXIV, Alcoholic Beverages and Tobacco §§ 561.29, 561.665] *to permit any contest or promotion or other form of recreational activity involving exploitation endangering the health, safety, and welfare of any person with dwarfism.*

The bravado ended when the radio station cancelled the dwarf-tossing contest. But the DJ was livid and threatened to sue the state of Florida again. Thankfully, his plan was stymied when the Florida Department of Business and Professional Regulation (DBPR) removed the likelihood of successful litigation. In May 2002, the DBPR published a Notice of Proposed Rulemaking that became effective on August 21, 2002.[6] The penalties for violating the dwarf-tossing law included license revocation or suspension, a civil fine not to exceed $1,000, or both.[7]

Chapter 13

A Perennial Weed

A Zeal for Repeal

Dwarf tossing feels like a perennial weed that just won't go away. And you never know who will sow the seeds of the next infestation—a business promoter, a dwarf wanting to be tossed, a radio station seeking publicity, or a lawyer challenging the constitutionality of the law banning such exploitation in licensed establishments. I never imagined it would be a state representative labeling the law as unnecessary.

Florida State Representative Ritch Workman added himself to the list of weed carriers in 2011 by introducing House Bill (HB) 4063 to repeal the 1989 Florida law banning dwarf tossing in establishments licensed to serve alcohol. Workman had a reputation as having "a zeal for repeal."[1] His hobby was perusing law books to identify anachronistic laws. For example, he had previously proposed repeal of state laws that required bicycle riders to keep one hand on the handlebars at all times and prohibited having a beer bottle collection in your home.[2] In Workman's mind, the restriction on dwarf tossing was on the list of obsolete laws that should be repealed.

In further support of the repeal, Workman maligned the Florida ban as Big Brother government restricting job opportunities for little people.[3] His timing was phenomenal.

Workman filed his repeal bill on October 3, 2011,[4] at the beginning of Dwarfism Awareness Month.

What was he thinking? Although he said the timing of his repeal bill was pure coincidence, clearly Workman wasn't thinking at all. Nevertheless, he quickly learned that Dwarfism Awareness Month was a time for LPA to raise positive awareness around dwarfism, address common misconceptions, and increase opportunities for people with dwarfism around the country.[5]

Resistance Team Action

The repeal bill sent the wrong message and stirred up little people against Workman's extraordinary show of ignorance. I was ready with a completed chronicle of LPA's successful advocacy against dwarf tossing in Florida and New York in 1989 and 1990, respectively. LPA national and Florida leadership were also ready and able to resist Workman's assault.

Despite being extremely aggravated at the prospect of having to repeat the fight against this obscenity, Robert and I signed on as members of the resistance team.[6] The team engaged all options—a letter-writing campaign, an online petition, letters from disability organizations, media interviews, letters to the editor, blog posts, monitoring the legislative agenda, and meeting with Florida state legislators in Tallahassee. LPA Advocacy Director Joe Stramondo rallied the team by signing off his October 8, 2011, email, "Fight to win!"

In a personal email the next day, Joe thanked me for helping to guide the team and wrote:

> *This sort of struggle is personal for us [. . .]*
> *This is a blessing [. . .] because it means that*
> *we fight that much harder than [ideologue*

*politicians] do, but a curse because we feel
the pain all the way down deep in our bones
when we have to fight for our basic dignity as
human beings.*[7]

Regular conference calls and group emails served to keep the resistance team on the same page for strategy, messaging, timing, and advocacy assignments. These calls also helped to energize us. Our resistance was resolute despite individual burdens of heavy workloads, a funeral, and surgery.

The resistance team urged LPA members and allies to do two things: (1) sign an online petition against HB 4063 at change.org; and (2) contact Workman to demand that he withdraw the bill. In a brilliant move, Joe set up the petition so that Workman received an email every time someone signed it. His computer actually pinged with each signature! It's easy to imagine that he went to sleep at night with the sound of pinging in his ears. The initial target was 3,000 signatures, but when more than 500 people signed in only seven hours, Joe raised the goal to 4,000.

On the same day the petition was uploaded, Executive Director Joanna Campbell issued LPA's official statement on the proposed bill informing the media and LPA members why we opposed the repeal.[8] In addition to highlighting the safety issues, LPA's statement showed how dwarf tossing objectifies the entire dwarf community. LPA President Gary Arnold put it this way:

*The individual who is tossed is like a shot
put or a javelin thrown in a track and field
event. Far from participants, dwarf tossing
treats people of short stature as a piece of*

equipment and encourages the general atti-
tude that people with dwarfism are objects.

Leah Smith, LPA VP of public relations, added:

In a day and age when society is confront-
ing bullying, it is a shame that this bill takes
us backwards. It enables bullying.

Media and Individual Appeals

In a separate call to action, Workman's contact information was shared with LPA members and allies so they could
urge him to preserve the safety and dignity of people with
dwarfism and the entire community. My October email to
Workman—

— recited the reasons for passage of the Florida law
  in 1989 as it appeared he hadn't read the legislative history.

— reminded him that the state of Florida has the police power to protect the health, safety, and morals of its citizens and that his bill violated Florida's duty to protect citizens with dwarfism.

— warned him that if his repeal bill passed and dwarf
  tossing were to return to Florida, his name would
  be forever linked to one of the ten worst inventions of the millennium.[9]

— asked him to do the honorable thing and withdraw
  the repeal bill for the sake of people with dwarfism, the state of Florida, and his own reputation.

In addition to direct communication with Workman,

LPA used media and online opportunities. For example, after the *Huffington Post* reported Workman's bill to repeal the dwarf-tossing ban in licensed establishments,[10] an editor invited LPA to submit a blog post giving LPA's viewpoint. LPA President Gary gave me the honor of writing this post.

Although this was my first time writing for a blog, I wasn't at a loss for words. Along with addressing the issues of exploitation, employment, entertainment, environment, and equality, I made the following statements:

- A career in dwarf tossing is likely to secure the tossee a check from the Social Security Administration or a plot in the cemetery.

- Before Florida passed the dwarf-tossing law in 1989, the environment became so toxic that children and adult little people feared "copycat" behavior and being thrown against their will.

- Dwarf tossing is offensive by any standard of human decency. A morally bankrupt practice, it disregards the value of people made in God's image.

The fear of dwarf-tossing copycats was not unfounded. Indeed, British actor, Martin Henderson, was thrown against his will in October 2011. According to news reports:

> *He was partially paralyzed on his birthday when a stranger lifted and heaved him onto the hard ground outside an English pub.*[11]

The incident went viral when actor Peter Dinklage used his 2012 Golden Globe Best Supporting Actor acceptance speech for his role in *Game of Thrones* to raise awareness about Henderson's injury.[12]

A few days after my blog post, Bill Klein took advantage of his celebrity status as a co-star in The Learning Channel's reality show, *The Little Couple.* He wrote a blog post in which he classified dwarf tossing as immoral, dangerous, bully behavior:

> *There is a driving force that separates us from all other creatures on this planet: morality. For the most part, we all understand the difference between right and wrong. Please remind (hopefully soon to be former) Representative Workman of what direction his [moral] compass should point.*[13]

Klein also challenged Workman's claim that the repeal would provide employment opportunities:

> *Job growth will not be addressed by removing a ban that protects the welfare and dignity of a population of people. Civil liberties are not put at risk by upholding the ban, but are supported by it. While one little person might seek to be the 'participant' in dwarf tossing, many others will continue to be ridiculed, objectified, and denied employment due to their association with this sort of behavior. Condoning it hurts our ability as a community to develop worthwhile, life-long careers that bring more than a foggy remembrance of a drunken night at a bar.*[14]

Turning up the Temperature

After a month of relentless advocacy appeals from the disability community and an onslaught of negative media attention, Workman still refused to withdraw HB 4063. As a result, November 14, 2011, was the date LPA chose to turn up the temperature. The 146 printed pages of the change.org petition was delivered to Workman's office with 4,834 signatures from people in 49 states, plus Puerto Rico and the District of Columbia, including 485 Floridians and 764 people from 27 countries.[15]

Workman also received a powerful joint letter from LPA President Gary Arnold and Mark Perriello, president of the American Association of People with Disabilities. The letter declared:

> [. . .] a show of solidarity on behalf of countless [people] with and without disabilities who are outraged at this repeal proposal. We urge you to withdraw this bill from consideration and rethink your blatant disregard for the human dignity of people with dwarfism.[16]

The two presidents made a strong case against harmful stereotypes that often marginalize even the most highly qualified and educated people with dwarfism as they try to enter the mainstream employment market. They demanded that Workman withdraw the bill that would legalize "the exploitation and abuse of persons with dwarfism" adding that "passing your bill would give state protection to perhaps the most grotesque example of such treatment to arise in modern times."[17]

Meetings with Representatives at State Capitol

While the resistance team was urging Workman to withdraw the repeal bill and pressuring him in the media, we also were monitoring the legislative process. We paid particular attention to the Business and Consumer Affairs Subcommittee to which the bill was assigned. Although HB 4063 wasn't on the agenda for the subcommittee meeting on December 6, 2011, we asked if it would be discussed at future meetings and were assured that it would never see the light of day.

An image of the words to the Preamble of the Florida Constitution etched below the railing on the second floor rotunda in the historic Capitol building.

In providential timing, I was in Tallahassee for meetings on December 7 and 8, 2011, as a member of the Florida Independent Living Council (FILC).[18] Part of FILC's agenda that week included visits to Florida state representatives to deliver our platform for the legislative session beginning in

January 2012. Opposition to the HB 4063 repeal bill was in the FILC platform. Our visit on Pearl Harbor Day, December 7, 2011, was symbolic—Workman's October attack had activated people with dwarfism and their allies to enter the fight with all guns blazing.

The first priority of the FILC delegation was to visit Representative Holder, the chair of the Business and Consumer Affairs Subcommittee. We went straight to his office fully prepared with an education folder that denounced Workman's repeal bill.[19] Holder and his chief policy aide greeted us with the good news that the bill wouldn't be placed on the subcommittee agenda—the bill would die in committee.

Buoyed by the good news, we went on to meet with Workman to see if he was ready to withdraw the bill. Workman's aide couldn't even look me in the eye and tried to block us from meeting with him. But after we indicated our willingness to wait all afternoon, if necessary, Workman finally invited us into his office. He appeared nervous and somewhat embarrassed—an appropriate reaction in the presence of a FILC delegation of five, including two LPA past presidents, Robert and myself.

We didn't need to debate the demerits of the repeal bill with Workman. He had been overwhelmed with the response from the LPA petition, letters, and media attention.

When we mentioned that the petition had over 4,800 signatures, he said, "Is that all? Every time someone signed, I got an email."

In response to media speculation that Workman had introduced his bill without talking to any little people, I asked him if he had ever met a little person. His answer was stunning—Robert and I made it two! In other words, he started this whole mess without even knowing a single person with dwarfism.

Although Workman refused to withdraw the bill, he made a written commitment not to promote the bill in any way. He said he had stayed away from the media for three weeks on this bill and believed that if he withdrew the bill as we requested, it would start a new round of media attention he didn't want to happen. Workman explained that despite his principled belief that the dwarf-tossing law violates individual rights, on balance he wasn't going to advance his principles if it meant returning little people to the era of circus-show entertainment of the 1930s. He disclosed that those who influenced him the most were the many parents and grandparents who spoke on behalf of their family members.

In his January 3, 2012, letter to the FILC president, Workman wrote:

> *I have made it a goal of mine for some time that I would try to repeal any laws that inhibit personal freedoms of Floridians. Although I find the activity of dwarf tossing disgusting, I do not believe little people should be singled out and treated any differently than everyone else. With that said, I realize that this bill has set back little people decades by bringing up the "freak show" image that dwarf tossing brings with it. This has caused more damage than good, and the bad outweighs the positive intent I had when filing this bill.*

As a direct result of LPA advocacy against Workman's repeal bill, it officially died in committee on March 9, 2012.[20] When the Florida legislative session ended in April, we proclaimed our victory.

Appendix B

Small Minds Look Down on Dwarfs

—Van Etten, C. Angela. Letter to the Editor, *Wall Street Journal*, November 22, 1985.

I feel compelled to add my sentiments to the European outcry about the [dwarf-tossing] spectacle. Like Lenny, I am a dwarf. However, unlike Lenny, I do not enjoy being thrown around. I can't imagine how Lenny could agree to becoming a human projectile or understand why the public would derive any pleasure from watching a man be thrown like a lifeless object. I wish someone could tell me that the Journal had mistakenly printed this from a book of seventeenth century history.

However, at 32 years of age, I have lived enough to know that it is not unusual for dwarfs of the 20th century to be treated as objects of ridicule, disrespect, and discrimination. We are laughed at by groups of children on the street; we are treated like children, instead of being given the respect that our adult years and appearance command; we are refused jobs, despite having prepared ourselves with a college education.

Yet dwarfs, who in the US mostly prefer to be called little people, have the same aspirations and abilities as other people. Our small bodies do not reflect the size of our minds or talent. Our similarities to the average-sized population far outnumber the superficial differences of our appearance.

I'd like to see two things happen; first, that the public

join the outcry against the depraved practice of dwarf tossing; and second, that the public put a stop to the practice
of throwing dwarfs into the endless arena of ridicule, disrespect, and discrimination. I know which one will take the
longest.

Appendix C

John Stossel Compromises Dwarfs in Name of Freedom

—Van Etten, C. Angela. **March 2002 post on LPA dwarfism listserv and website, https://lpaonline.org.**

John Stossel used freedom to justify his views on dwarf tossing. He promoted David Flood's freedom of choice to control his own body. He argued that everyone's freedom would eventually be taken if activists get to decide for everyone. However, if freedom and individual liberty were truly Stossel's concern, he would have been equally concerned to protect the freedom of little people other than David Flood. Instead, Stossel elevated Flood's freedom to participate in suicidal, violent entertainment in a manner that imprisons other little people in an image that is demeaning and dehumanizing.

Yes, Flood is free to choose employment that is dangerous. Likewise, we as activist little people are free to lobby for the children and other adult little people who will suffer at the hand of copycat bullies.

Yes, Flood is free to stand in a bar and offer himself as a human projectile. Likewise, we as activist little people are free to denounce a practice that encourages the public to ridicule and discriminate against all little people in public places.

Yes, Flood is free to prostitute his services as a tossee. Likewise, we as activist little people are free to appeal to the conscience of every decent American to not become the "John" and invite Flood into their bedroom.

Yes, Flood is free to promote a morally bankrupt practice that disregards the value of man—made in the image of God. Likewise, we as activist little people are free to advance the view that all people are valued by God and should be honored and respected accordingly.

Yes, Flood is free to capitalize on his God-given attributes. Likewise, we as activist little people are free to argue that Flood has sold out by using his body for an activity that discredits his true aspirations to be an entertainer and actor. We prefer to capitalize on our God-given intelligence, personality, and skills.

Yes, Flood is free to protest a law that bans dwarf tossing. Likewise, we as activist little people are free to defend a law that bans dwarf tossing for all the reasons stated above. State legislators are also free to pass laws that protect the health, safety, welfare, and morals of their citizens. The Florida dwarf-tossing ban is such a law.

Regrettably, in order for John Stossel to bolster his libertarian argument against a dwarf-tossing ban, he sacrificed a fundamental freedom—freedom of speech. Robert and Angela were free to speak against dwarf tossing with Stossel on tape for about 30 minutes. But in making his case, Stossel did some tossing of his own. He tossed out the discussion showing that dwarf tossing is a balance between Flood's right to control his own body and the right of other little people not to be tossed in the garbage along with him.

Stossel also compromised his integrity as a journalist when he accepted David Flood at his word. He disregarded the danger this practice poses for Flood. He portrayed the practice as no more risky than boxing, football, and fashion modeling. A responsible journalist would have learned that it is much more risky for David to be thrown. A responsible journalist would have learned that Flood's career in dwarf tossing is likely to secure him a Social Security disability check or a plot in the cemetery, not a lifestyle of the rich and famous.

Busybody, activist—whatever Stossel wants to call us, we remain free to advance the right of little people to be treated with respect, dignity, and equality.

So if the Son makes you free, you will be free indeed.
~ John 8:36, NASB

Appendix D

Disability Coalition Against Dwarf Tossing

Access Center for Independent Living, Ohio
Access Living, Chicago, Illinois
ADAPT Chicago
ADAPT Montana
American Association of People with Disabilities
American Council of the Blind
American Public Health Association, Disability Section
Association of Programs for Rural Independent Living, Arizona
Autistic Self Advocacy Network
Brazoria County Center for Independent Living, Texas
California Foundation for Independent Living Centers
Center for Independent Living of South Florida, Inc.
Coalition for Independent Living Options, Inc.
Coalition of Texans with Disabilities
Community Resources for Independent Living, California
Disability Resource Association
Disability Resource Initiative, Kentucky
Disability Rights Oregon
Disability Rights Education & Defense Fund
Disability Rights Florida
Disability Solutions for Independent Living, Daytona Beach, Florida
Equal Rights Center, Washington, DC

Florida Independent Living Council (FILC)
Fort Bend Center for Independent Living, Texas
Houston Center for Independent Living
Illinois/Iowa Center for Independent Living
Illinois Network of Centers for Independent Living
Illinois Valley Center for Independent Living
JJ's List
Liberty Resources, Philadelphia, Pennsylvania
LPA national and Florida chapters
National Action Network, Kansas Chapter
National Association of the Deaf
National Coalition for Mental Health Recovery
National Council on Independent Living
National Federation of the Blind
National Organization of Nurses with Disabilities
New York Association on Independent Living
Not Dead Yet
Placer Independent Resource Services, Inc., California
Progress Center for Independent Living
Resource Center for Accessible Living, Inc., New York
Silicon Valley Independent Living Center
Southeast Alaska Independent Living
Southern Tier Independence Center, New York
Tri-County Patriots for Independent Living, Washington
United Spinal Association
Wisconsin Coalition of Independent Living Centers

PART III

Equal
Access

Chapter 14

Let Me Ride

Action Principles Clash

I confess to being an Alinsky trainee dropout. As a resident alien in the United States, I wasn't ready to risk deportation in 1984 for participating in an action to disrupt rush hour traffic on Pennsylvania Avenue in front of the White House. I declined to join would-be bus riders with walkers, canes, and wheelchairs in surrounding and stopping buses from moving for an hour. Rather than be arrested, I watched from the sidewalk and informed a bus driver what was happening.

So how did I get from Cleveland, Ohio, to standing on the sidewalk in front of the White House in Washington, DC? As a board member of the Services for Independent Living in the Cleveland suburb of Euclid, I was eager to learn how to bring accessible mass transit to Cleveland. As a result, I signed up for training with American Disabled for Accessible Public Transit (ADAPT)—an organization that had successfully lobbied for accessible mass transit in Denver, Colorado—to lobby for a federal law that would require all new public buses be lift-equipped and accessible to people with mobility impairments.

The ADAPT trainers were nondisabled community organizers who followed Saul Alinsky's methods expressed in his 1971 book, *Rules for Radicals*. In Alinsky style, the organizers appealed to the self-interest of our disenfranchised group of people with mobility impairments and a legitimate grievance about the lack of accessible mass transit. They agitated the group by rubbing resentments and fanning hostilities.[1] I could see that this was designed to get people to participate, attack apathy, and disturb the complacency where people had simply come to accept a situation.[2] Even so, I wasn't one to accept an unjust situation and was neither apathetic nor complacent.

Before going to the ADAPT training, I had never heard of Saul Alinsky. Nonetheless it didn't take long before my moral values chafed against two Alinksy fundamentals: (1) *"an organizer does not have a fixed truth*—truth to him is relative and changing;"[3] and (2) the real and only question regarding the ethics of means and ends is whether "this particular end justifies this particular means."[4]

Although I wholeheartedly agreed that action was necessary so that people with mobility impairments could ride the bus, I totally disagreed that this end justified jettisoning truth, respect, and dignity of people with disabilities.

During a meeting with Transportation Secretary Elizabeth Dole, I saw another Alinsky rule in action: "Whenever possible, go outside the expertise of the enemy."[5] With the purpose of increasing Dole's insecurity, anxiety, and uncertainty, ADAPT protestors encircled her in the meeting room. She was clearly uncomfortable with not being able to make eye contact with people. ADAPT's assigned spokesperson was a little person who abandoned her dignity and bopped from her wheelchair to sit on the tabletop to present the groups demands. I had failed in my prior attempt to convince this woman she was being manipulated and that the accessible mass transit end didn't justify this means.

My discomfort with ADAPT's use of Alinsky's methods

was a primary reason I dropped out of the ADAPT training three days early, but foreboding news about Robert's job also made it clear Robert needed me more at that moment. Nonetheless, advocating for equal access in mass transit remained on my radar.

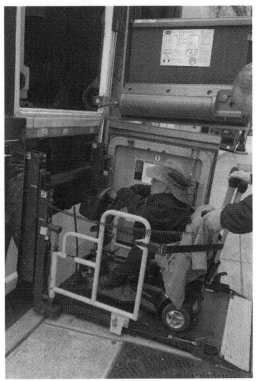

Robert Van Etten seated in his scooter on a vertical lift at the back of a tour bus with the operator behind him holding the lift button in his left hand and resting his hand on the top of Robert's crutches in their holder on the back of the scooter.

When we moved from Cleveland, Ohio, to Rochester, New York, a few months later, Robert was the first one to pick up the mantle as a member of the Coalition for Accessible Transit. In June 1988, we both picketed with coalition members outside a downtown shopping plaza to protest inaccessible public transportation. Robert was the spokesperson on the evening news and voiced support for the New York state bill that would require transit authorities to add wheelchair lifts to new buses when using state funds to make the purchase.

Angela Van Etten exiting a New York City bus—marked with the international access symbol—riding her scooter down the ramp followed by her brother-in-law, Rob Coote.

In July 1990, the ADA federal civil rights disability law expanded to all states the requirement that all new mass transit buses have wheelchair lifts without regard to the funding source. During the 18-month education period prior to the ADA's effective date in January 1992, I got to dive deep into the new law when I wrote the ADA chapter on transportation in the *Americans with Disabilities: Practice and Compliance Manual.*[6] From 1991 to 1995, Robert served on the Rochester-Genesee Regional Transportation Authority Accessible Transportation Committee by appointment of New

York Governor Mario Cuomo. The committee was charged with monitoring ADA compliance in the eight-county area in and around Rochester for lifts on new buses and the complementary paratransit, door-to-door service for people with disabilities who are unable to use fixed route transportation for some or all of their trips.

No Wheelchairs Allowed

In May 1993, a cheetah responded to Robert's call and the two fixed eyes on one another until the first one blinked. Happily, the fence separating them at the zoo made the outcome mere table talk for Robert rather than table food for the cheetah. But Robert going eye-to-eye with the cheetah was less chilling than going head-to-head with the zoo's manager.

This happened during what had been planned as a relaxing day between business trips— I would be in St. Louis, Missouri, and Robert was headed to Minneapolis, Minnesota. Instead, our visit to the world-famous St. Louis Zoo almost got us arrested as we tried to board the zoo-line railroad. We had looked forward to using both the train and Robert's wheelchair to reduce walking between the zoo's exhibits. The sign posted at the railroad station telegraphed trouble ahead:

> OUR INSURANCE PROHIBITS
> WHEELCHAIRS OR STROLLERS
> ON THE TRAIN.
> ONLY FOLDED UMBRELLA
> STROLLERS ARE ALLOWED.

Because this was a clear violation of the ADA, we photographed the sign and stayed in line determined to ride with

Robert's wheelchair. When we got to the front of the line, Robert wheeled onto the platform only to be told that he must leave the wheelchair at the station. The attendant had no interest in Robert saying he needed the wheelchair when he got off the train. She was adamant he leave the wheelchair behind. We asked to see the manager when she wouldn't budge. She was unimpressed when I told her that refusal to allow Robert to bring the wheelchair on the train was an ADA violation.

Meanwhile we blocked the path of people waiting to board the train. Not wanting to inconvenience these people any longer than necessary, we agreed to step aside while we waited for the manager. When several trains came and went with no arrival of a manager, the need to take further action was evident.

We moved back to the front of the line with the intent of boarding the next train with the wheelchair. I made a speech to the people waiting in line behind us and explained that our civil right to ride the train as equal members of society was being violated. There was only one problem— we needed help lifting the wheelchair onto the train. This problem was solved when a man in the line agreed to load the wheelchair.

When the next train pulled into the station, we moved onto the platform ready to board with our helper toting the wheelchair. The plan was thwarted when several zoo security staff surrounded us, blocked our attempt to board, and ordered us off the platform so that the train could leave the station.

Now we had a choice to make. We could cause the trains to stop running by refusing to leave the platform and be arrested for refusing to move. The alternative was to step aside again based on the assurance that the manager was on his way. We chose to be reasonable and moved off the platform so that the train could leave. Even so, we tried to keep the pressure on by blocking the front of the line so that no one could board incoming trains. But this plan was foiled when staff began loading trains from the other end of the line.

It took another 30 minutes for the zoo manager to show up. We were grateful that he recognized separating Robert from his wheelchair was against the law. Even though he wouldn't allow the wheelchair on the train, the manager offered an acceptable alternative accommodation. We rode the train and watched the wheelchair ride in a separate vehicle alongside the train.

We declined the manager's offer of a designated driver to ride us around the zoo in an electric cart. A principle was at stake. We didn't want special treatment. Our only desire was to ride on the train like everyone else. Nonetheless we accepted a cart ride to the sea lion show as compensation for the delay caused by denying us access to the train.

Taxis Refuse Rides with Scooter

Calling 911 wasn't in our plan the night of LPA's 60th anniversary banquet in Denver, Colorado, in July 2017. But hotel security staff supplied an oxygen tank, and Robert was rushed to the Denver Health Medical Center in an ambulance where he was admitted to the ICU in respiratory distress.

Although I followed in a taxi, the driver would have refused to take me and my scooter if not for the Sheraton hotel security supervisor reminding him of the contract Yellow Cab had with the hotel. Indeed, the supervisor was so disturbed by how poorly the cab driver treated me that rather than leave me to the mercy of Yellow Cab on my return in the early hours of the morning, she came to the hospital at 2:00 a.m. to give me a ride back to the hotel. When my scooter wouldn't fit in her trunk, she got help to lift it onto the back seat of her car.

Even though Sheraton security staff gave me taxi vouchers to use when visiting Robert at the hospital, they were of little use when calling for a ride back to the hotel. Multiple cab drivers refused to transport me with my scooter. One night it took me two hours to get a taxi. The first driver took one look at the scooter and drove off.

When I called Yellow Cab to report this incident, the dispatcher said I had to order an accessible cab if I had a scooter. When I asked how long an accessible cab would take to arrive, the dispatcher wouldn't give me a straight answer. Upon further prodding, the dispatcher disclosed there was no guarantee that an accessible cab would pick me up at all. He admitted that the day before, eight riders who called for an accessible cab never got a ride.

Some other little people attending the Denver conference were also stranded when Yellow Cab refused to pick them up when they saw their scooter or wheelchair. It's bad enough to be stuck at home, but quite another to be stranded and unable to get home.

Each night I left Robert in the ICU after a day of medical staff giving him breathing treatments and diagnostic tests to rule out any catastrophic causes of his respiratory problem. Each night I was tearful and distraught outside on the sidewalk as I watched cabs coming and going without accepting my fare. If it had been daylight, and if my scooter had GPS, and if it had been in a safe neighborhood—I would have scootered back to the hotel on my own wheels. But that wasn't an option in the dark in an unfamiliar, rough part of town.

I called out to God daily for both of us and was grateful that others aware of the situation were also praying. Word spread like wildfire at the LPA conference that Robert went to the hospital in an ambulance. When Stacie Nichols-Pouliot saw me in the lobby the next morning she told me that she and Roger were praying for us. I had also alerted church friends via text of our immediate need for prayer support.

After two-and-a-half days in the hospital, the doctors determined that the most likely cause of Robert's breathing issue was the cumulative effect of being in the Mile High City for a week. As a sea level resident of Florida, Robert was classified as a flatlander. The medical consensus was that he would be fine once he got back to sea level. But in order to get home safely, he traveled with a portable oxygen concentrator.

The taxi issue was resolved by connecting with a private transportation operator servicing the Sheraton. After identifying a reliable and helpful operator, I got his number and made reservations with him to pick us up when Robert was discharged from the hospital and when we needed a ride to the airport.

All credit goes to God for taking care of us both during this stressful time.

> *When I was desperate, I called out,*
> *and God got me out of a tight spot.*
> *God's angel sets up a circle of protection*
> *around us while we pray.*
> *~ Psalm 34:6-7, Message*

Chapter 15

Breaking the Six-Inch Reach Barrier

Desperate Moves to Access ATMs

The bank was closed on the weekend, we needed cash, and at 54 inches the ATM was out of Robert's reach. Not deterred by a six-inch reach barrier, he backed up our Honda wagon to the ATM, opened the hatchback and stood on the bumper. Mission accomplished, or so he thought. A police officer stopped him from leaving the scene after witnessing his suspicious behavior.

After seeing that Robert hadn't emptied all of the ATM cash into the trunk, the officer let him off with a warning, "Don't do this again."

So what were little people supposed to do to gain access to ATMs? The federal Access Board—responsible for setting accessibility standards under the ADA—seemed like a good place to start.

Robert and I were among the 700 LPA members and associates who responded to the Access Board's call for public comments on the height of ATMs. In LPA's 1993 letter-writing campaign led by Nancy Mayeux—a Florida parent of two children with dwarfism—members asked for ATMs to be lowered six inches, from 54 to 48 inches. However, LPA's hopes for equal access under the ADA were dashed on July 15, 1993.

The powerful banking industry persuaded the Access

Board to allow operable parts on ATMs to remain out of reach at 54 inches. The board cited the need for further research on the reach range of little people and the implications for taller people. The blow was devastating. *How would we ever achieve independence if the Access Board was more willing to accommodate the banking industry than the people who use their equipment?*

LPA Membership on ANSI Access Committee

One year later, LPA learned that a better place to start was the ICC/ANSI A117.1 Committee on Accessible and Usable Buildings and Facilities. LPA had never heard of it until John Salmen—an architect member representing the American Hotel and Lodging Association—approached LPA President Ruth Ricker in July 1994. John explained that the ANSI Access Committee produced the equivalent of a model building code making public buildings and facilities accessible to people with disabilities.[1] John knew that the 700 letters from LPA members to the federal Access Board hadn't achieved the desired result and encouraged LPA not to give up. He revealed that the ANSI Access Committee was ready to hear about the access needs of little people and nudged LPA to apply for membership in the category designated for users requiring accessibility.[2]

President Ruth accepted John's advice that the beginning of the ANSI Access Committee five-year revision cycle of the model code was the perfect time for LPA to submit proposed changes. Thus she obtained LPA Board approval to apply for membership. Now all Ruth needed was to appoint a delegate to represent LPA at the meetings.

Ruth offered me this assignment given my background as an attorney and advocate. I didn't doubt my qualifications, but I did question the volunteer assignment given the enormity of the charge. The six-inch reach barrier applied not only to ATMs, but also to bathrooms, elevator buttons, public telephones, gas pumps, door and window handles, laundry and kitchen appliances—everything open to the public activated with a push, pull or turn.

Robert forewarned me about the difficulty of the task, but LPA's recent advocacy defeat on the height of ATMs was fresh on my mind. He remembered the telephone industry's successful opposition to lowering the height of public pay phones when he worked for the federal Access Board as a communications engineer in 1981.

But ringing in my ears was the question of Ginny, a teenage little person in one of my LPA advocacy workshops, "Who is going to do something about the height of ATMs?"

At the time, I had no answer for Ginny. Now I had no answer for President Ruth when she said, "If you don't do it, Angela, who will?"

In prayerfully weighing my decision, I focused on two facts: (1) the civil right of people with dwarfism to full and equal enjoyment of public buildings and facilities; and (2) my dwarfism experience and advocacy training which had prepared me to be the one to make our right a reality.

Not finding anyone else lining up to tackle the giant, I saw it as a calling from God to accept the position of LPA's delegate to the ANSI Access Committee.

LPA's membership application to the ANSI Access Committee was approved on September 9, 1994, and so my work began. Despite my credentials for the position, I still had a huge learning curve. I not only had to learn the ANSI process, but also to understand how to connect with the interests of committee members who were outside my sphere of influence: building owners and operators, manufacturers, representatives of regulatory agencies, and building code officials. I also didn't know how I would balance the demands on my time with work and the physical demands of flying thousands of miles on the many trips between our residence in Rochester, New York, and ANSI Committee meetings in Washington, DC, in all kinds of weather conditions. At least finances weren't an issue—LPA paid my travel expenses.

Response to Call for Data

With initial guidance from John Salmen, LPA began with ten proposed changes targeting the six-inch reach range barrier in the ANSI access standard. Although the committee was sympathetic, in March 1995 most members opposed such a drastic change without statistical data supporting LPA's proposals. To move the committee members from sympathy to code changes, LPA needed answers to legitimate questions:

- Is 48 inches the right height?

- How high can little people reach?

- What effect will this have on people with other disabilities?

- How much will this cost?

The July 1995 LPA national conference in Denver was perfectly timed for gathering the statistical data to answer these questions. So the LPA Measure-Up Campaign was born. Robert, a rehabilitation engineer and former president of LPA, partnered with Dr. Ed Steinfeld, an architect and ANSI Committee member, to design a reach range survey. One hundred subjects would have made the survey statistically valid, which we well surpassed since the campaign captured the measurements of 172 adult little people.[3] The reward of Hershey chocolate may have induced some to line up at Robert's Adaptive Living table at the LPA Expo for measurements of their height, arm extension, eye height, and vertical reach, but the desire to use ATMs was a greater motivation.

The reach range survey documented that if the unobstructed reach standard was reduced to 48 inches about 80% of people with dwarfism would be able to reach ATMs and everything else activated with a push, pull, or turn. Unfortunately, the raw data from the LPA Measure-Up Campaign in Denver couldn't be analyzed in time for consideration at the July 1995 ANSI Access Committee meeting. Rather, the data was used to support LPA's 48-inch proposal at the February 1996 ANSI Access Committee meeting going through the second draft of proposed revisions to the ANSI Access Code. Committee members representing other disability organizations were also key players in supporting this change. [4]

In the past, calls for more research had been sufficient to ward off any moves for code revisions. But LPA's research results pulled the rug out from under those determined to keep the status quo. My strategy of sitting next to different committee members at each ANSI Access Committee meeting (which lasted from one to three consecutive days) also gave me plenty of time to personalize the issue for those inclined to oppose any change to the reach range standard. For example, I asked the delegate representing the physical therapy association why she was voting with industry members against lowering the unobstructed side-reach range to 48 inches rather than standing up for the patients she purported to represent. For those entrenched in their opposition, I listened to their objections and prepared counter-arguments.

Committee Debates, Public Comments, and Federal Access Board

After a vigorous debate in February 1996, the ANSI Access Committee agreed to break the six-inch reach barrier. Jubilation, triumph, joy, exhilaration, satisfaction, victory. The unobstructed side reach[5] was lowered from 54 to 48 inches in the second draft revision of the ANSI Access Code. John Salmen characterized it as the biggest code change in 20 years. Another member said that LPA shamed ANSI Access Committee members into doing the right thing. Whatever the reason, I discerned that God was at work.

I celebrated the moment despite knowing there was a long way to go before the decision was final. There would be yet another call for public comments on the final draft of the ANSI Access Code. This would likely include further objections to the change from 54 to 48 inches. Then ANSI Access Committee members would be balloted for approval of the entire document.

Meanwhile, those industries affected by the change made moves to carve out exceptions. For instance, the elevator industry was generally willing to meet the 48 inches but sought an exception for buildings with more than 16 elevator stops. The ANSI Access Committee approved this exception with LPA's acquiescence.[6] The banking industry fought hard for an ATM exception. But unlike the elevator industry, the bankers had been on notice since a 1992 federal rulemaking that little people—and more than half a million other people whose disability involved a reach limitation—couldn't use ATMs with operable parts as high as 54 inches.[7] The committee voted unanimously not to offer an exception for ATMs. Another battle won.

The federal Access Board provided further evidence that the time was right for breaking the six-inch reach barrier.

The Access Board reviewed the ADA Accessibility Guidelines (ADAAG) while the ANSI Access Committee revised the ANSI Access Code. The goal was to harmonize the two codes by eliminating the differences between ADAAG and ANSI. This offered a huge bonus for LPA looking to eliminate height discrimination under federal, state, and local laws.

After receiving an inside tip that the ADAAG Advisory Committee was tentative about recommending a reduction from 54 to 48 inches, Robert and I drove almost 400 miles from Rochester, New York, to Washington, DC. On July 7, 1996, we both made public comments to the ADAAG Advisory Committee in favor of breaking the six-inch reach barrier. We repeated the civil rights argument given to the ANSI Access Committee along with providing research data, the trend of automated devices replacing personal services, technical feasibility, the social impact, and the contributions little people make to society. We spoke against little people accessing the built environment in a manner that is frequently demeaning, debilitating, dangerous, and perpetuating dependence. We celebrated another victory when the ADAAG Advisory Committee recommended the 48-inch change to the full Access Board.

One of the concerns of both the ADAAG Advisory Committee and ANSI's Access Committee was the lack of data on how high a little person can reach over an obstruction, such as a counter. Both committees expressed reservations about changing the unobstructed side reach height without also addressing the obstructed reach height. Some saw this as a reason for keeping the status quo until knowing all the data. Delay equaled denial. And LPA resolved to remove this excuse. At the Indianapolis LPA national conference in August 1996, we continued the Measure-Up Campaign to see how an obstruction affected the reach of people with dwarfism. This time—with the help of LPA member Alex Krywonos— we measured more than 200 little people.

In October 1996, I was back in Washington, DC for AN-SI's Access Committee meeting to consider the comments and negative ballots filed on the final draft document. My primary task was to defend retention of the 48-inch unobstructed side reach. At this stage in the revision cycle, I couldn't propose further changes based on the dramatic results of the 1996 obstructed reach survey in Indianapolis. But I could use the Indianapolis[8] data to show that the proposed six-inch reduction for the unobstructed side reach was tame in comparison to changes needed for an obstructed side reach. Once again LPA prevailed over the fierce opposition from the Building Owners and Manufacturer's Association (BOMA) and Bell Communications.

David and Goliath Battle

Never guilty of rushing to judgment, the ANSI Access Committee considered negative ballots and comments on a second public review of the final draft from April 30 to May 2, 1997. The American Bankers Association (ABA), a gas pump manufacturer, and the National Automatic Merchandising Association (representing vending machine manufacturers and operators) joined BOMA in opposition to the 48-inch unobstructed side reach. Given the size and economic power of these opponents, a David and Goliath battle was imminent. I used my usual arsenal of weapons: preparation, persuasion, and prayer.

Despite my six-page handout that systematically listed and answered every argument made by those opposing the reduction to 48 inches, it seemed there was no hope for change. Experienced disability advocates were concerned that our early victory was about to slip away. Delegates were under a lot of pressure to change their early votes in support of the change. But I believed God could move the hearts of ANSI Access Committee members to retain the 48-inch reach range.

After a five-hour battle and the longest debate on a single provision in the whole three-year revision cycle, the room was quiet as the votes were carefully counted: thirteen in favor of 54 inches, eighteen for 48 inches, and seven abstentions. Victory. I attributed the triumph to Divine intervention. *How else do you explain the force that withstood three of the most powerful industries in the nation—banking, oil, and retail?*

Even so, the victory wasn't absolute. The banking and gas pump industries succeeded in getting an exception to the 48-inch standard to permit existing elements to remain at 54 inches. This meant that unless a building element is being altered or moved, alterations that occur in the vicinity of the element don't trigger ANSI's alteration requirements. As a practical matter, this meant that equipment could remain in service and even be deployed to another location until the end of its life cycle which in the case of an ATM can be as long as 10 to 15 years.

The April/May 1997 ANSI Access Committee meeting should have ended this ANSI revision cycle.[9] However, in October 1997, consideration was given to public comments on the substantive changes to the second public review of the final draft, including the two exceptions to the 48-inch unobstructed side reach. I was distressed to learn that I not only had to argue against the industry exceptions, but also repeat the arguments for lowering the unobstructed side reach from 54 to 48 inches.

I hadn't prepared for this and didn't think I could handle going through yet another battle. In my anguish, I called Robert to put this on our church prayer chain. God was faithful, and the ANSI Access Committee chairperson limited the 54- to 48-inch debate to a recap of the main issues and only allowed the clock to run for one hour.

After the fifth and final debate on LPA's proposal, the victory was more decisive—twenty-two votes for 48 inches, eight votes for 54 inches and only two abstentions. But just as the ANSI Access Committee became more resolute in their decision to lower the unobstructed side reach, they also dug deeper on their resolve to permit an exception for existing elements. My motion to remove this exception was soundly defeated.

For the most part, little people and half a million other people whose disability involved a reach limitation could look forward to operable parts in public buildings and facilities being within reach in those jurisdictions adopting ANSI Access Code editions from 1998 and thereafter. Almost fifteen years have now passed, and the future is here. The six-inch unobstructed side reach barrier is broken in day-to-day use of public buildings and facilities built or altered since 1998.

Many little people have said they think of me every time they use an ATM, but I think of God's grace, power, and justice. He deserves the credit for making the impossible happen. My role was to be obedient to the calling and follow God's lead.

Chapter 16

Battle for Access in Different Forums

Federal Access Board

Unlike the 1999 preparation for potential disaster in Y2K, the preparation required to make the built environment more accessible to little people in the new millennium was more than an exercise. Little people—and a half million others whose disability involved a reach limitation—needed independent use of public facilities such as ATMs, bathrooms, elevators, gas pumps, and the like. Although the six-inch reach barrier was broken in the 1998 edition of the ICC/ANSI A117.1 Committee on Accessible and Usable Buildings and Facilities, more work was needed to effect change in federal law. As a result, I continued to advocate for independent access in my positions as vice chair[1] of ANSI's Access Committee and as chairperson of the LPA Access Committee.[2]

The testimony Robert and I made to the ADAAG Advisory Committee took three years to bear fruit. The day finally came on November 16, 1999, when the Access Board published in the Federal Register its Notice of Proposed Rulemaking to update ADAAG. This brought us a step closer to breaking the 48-inch reach barrier in federal law. For the six-month public comment period, I coordinated LPA's advocacy in support of lowering the unobstructed side-reach range from 54 to 48 inches.

LPA's 6,500 members and other disability organizations were encouraged to write letters to the federal Access Board.

In March 2000, I arranged for LPA members to give testimony at public hearings held in Los Angeles, California, and Arlington, Virginia.[3] In addition, I attended the ANSI Access Committee meeting in Rockville, Maryland, where it was decided that the ANSI Access Committee would make comments to the Access Board supporting 48 inches in ADAAG, the federal access code.

On May 15, 2000, I prepared and submitted LPA's official comments on the ADAAG rulemaking. The 25-page document was a culmination of my five years working on the ANSI Access Committee and took more than 45 hours to prepare. The Access Board later reported that several hundred comments addressed the merits of lowering the unobstructed side-reach range to 48 inches, but only mentioned two organizations by name—LPA and the ANSI Access Committee, both of which I was privileged to have led to this historic change.

After the closing of the public comment period, the Access Board held informational meetings on October 24-25, 2000, in Washington, DC. Their question was: "What effect would a 48-inch standard have on manufactured equipment and newly constructed building elements?" I represented LPA and recruited some local LPA members to be sure we had a strong presence.[4]

At the informational meeting, the ATM manufacturers made this stunning statement: "Our new generation of machines will meet the 48-inch standard." *Really?* For years they said this couldn't be done. To be sure we heard correctly, Access Board staff asked the manufacturers to repeat the statement. In a jaw-dropping moment—worthy of a ticker tape parade with fireworks, balloons, and the blowing of horns—the ATM manufacturers confirmed that their new generation of machines would meet the 48-inch standard.

Our jubilance couldn't even be dampened by the gas pump manufacturers' continued fight against change.

The gas pump representative asked the Access Board for exemption from the 48-inch reach provision they had successfully included in a draft version of the International Building Code (IBC). Naturally, I asked the Access Board to follow the ICC/ANSI standard, refuse the exemption, and not allow gas pumps to be installed at 54 inches.

Four years after the October 2000 meeting with the Access Board in Washington, DC, a final reach-range decision was published on July 23, 2004.[5] Euphoria barely described the joy of finally seeing the 48-inch standard accepted in the 2004 ADAAG federal standard. This was huge. We were no longer dependent on state and local building codes adopting the 1998 ANSI Access Code. The federal ADAAG law applied uniformly across the nation and was supreme. A state law could be more stringent than federal law, but couldn't require less than the federal law. In other words, the unobstructed 48-inch reach range applied across the entire nation.

At the same time, there was some letdown when gas pump manufacturers succeeded in their quest for an exception for machines installed on

Robert Van Etten stands next to an accessible gas pump with his head level with the left tail light on a Mazda 6 wagon and inserts his credit card into the machine with his left hand.

existing curbs. This exception allowed installation of operable parts on gas pumps as high as 54 inches. But as though God rewarded us for our efforts, a new accessible gas station was built about one mile from our home. In appreciation for compliance with this new building code provision, I carefully monitor my fuel gauge to be sure I fill up at this RaceTrac gas station.

International Building Code (IBC)

LPA needed to know and learn the process in various forums when advocating for equal access in public places. The gas pump manufacturers—after being denied an exemption in the ANSI Access Code—proposed an exemption in the 2000 IBC. LPA was unfamiliar with IBC process and had no budget to lobby against it.

Not so easily defeated, I recruited David Bradford, who was willing to attend the IBC conference in his hometown of Portland, Oregon. We boned up on the process, and David successfully argued for the removal of the exemption at the IBC hearing on March 25, 2001. Thus, the IBC required fuel hoses, fuel selection buttons, and credit card readers on new gas pumps to meet the 48-inch side- reach range standard.

This rattled the Gas Pump Manufacturers Association (GPMA) so much that they sent two attorney representatives to our home in Stuart, Florida, on May 15, 2001. They brought a proposal for LPA to consider. After indicating that a 48-inch design was in the works, they asked LPA to trust the industry to redesign equipment on their own undisclosed timetable. *Did they really think we were that naïve?* In effect, they were asking LPA to stay home and do nothing. I told the attorneys that this wasn't going to happen. Their only consolation prize was a seafood lunch in the sun on the Intra-coastal Waterway.

In 2002, David continued to represent LPA at IBC hearings in Pittsburgh, Pennsylvania, and Fort Worth, Texas, where he successfully held the line against repeated attempts to get a blanket exemption for gas pumps.

The National Elevator Industry

Angela Van Etten stands in front of an elevator panel of floor buttons and inserts a hotel keycard to access the elevator floor

When the National Elevator Industry Inc. (NEII) Task Group asked to meet with LPA representatives[6] in Delray Beach, Florida, in June 2001 and May 2002, they genuinely wanted to address our access issue. Despite having an exemption to the 48-inch reach requirement in elevators serving more than 16 openings,[7] the industry remained true to its 1996 commitment to explore ways of providing little people 100% elevator access in the future.

NEII came up with a technology solution designed to en-able little people to reach ANY floor destination. With technology comparable to setting the time on an alarm clock, a person would use an up or down scan button to select a floor destination. The scan button would be located adjacent to, or immediately above, the emergency control buttons at the bottom of the panel.[8]

Service Award

At the July 2001 annual LPA banquet in Toronto, Canada, I was stunned to receive the Kitchens Meritorious Service Award in recognition of my 20 years of service to LPA. In an appreciation article published in *LPA Today*, I credited God for achieving what appeared as insurmountable in overcoming the atrocity of dwarf tossing and breaking the six-inch reach barrier in public buildings and facilities. I encouraged LPA members to get involved, irrespective of the difficulty of the task or fear of failure:

> *Success is not measured by outcomes or how we compare with others. Rather, it is measured by how we use our God-given talents. We only fail when we squander our abilities and live to please ourselves.*

Little did I know how much work was left to be done.

Access in Public Bathrooms

My work on the ANSI Access Committee continued as chairperson of the Task Force on Obstructed Reach Range, Extremes of Physical Size. The task was daunting, but I continued to trust God to guide us towards improving access for little people in public bathrooms. Little people want to wash and dry their hands like everyone else.

The challenge was to find a solution that didn't deny access to wheelchair users who needed a 34-inch-tall lavatory/sink. At this height, little people can't reach faucets and soap dispensers set any farther back than 11 inches.[9] The solution suggested by industry consultants was to leave the lavatory at 34 inches and install faucets and soap dispensers within the accessible reach of 11 inches. This could be achieved with electronic activation or installation on the side rather than at the back of the sink.

On September 28, 2001, I submitted the task group report to the ANSI Access Committee with the recommended proposals for bathroom access. After following the many steps in the ANSI process, the proposal was approved as a revision to the 2003 ANSI Access standard.[10]

Change occurred as a result of caring enough to do something, commitment, choosing the right forum, collaborating with industry experts, clear communications, and confidence in God's ability to change hearts.

Angela Van Etten rinses her hands using a water flow activated by a sensor, but is unable to use soap because the soap dispenser is installed out of reach on the mirror.

Time to Pass the Baton to Another LPA Delegate

After serving as LPA's delegate on the ANSI Access Committee for eight years with 100% attendance at about 22 full committee meetings, the time was ripe to train my replacement. I didn't think LPA should be so dependent on one person to advocate for equal access.

My discovery of Tricia Mason, the LPA District 10 director, was exciting. She was perfect for the position. Tricia had advocacy skills, an interest in architecture and design, and her employment by the Wyoming Governor's Planning Council on Developmental Disabilities gave her some flexibility to attend meetings in Washington, DC. In December 2001, Tricia accepted the position as my alternate, and in February 2002 we traded places. I passed Tricia the delegate baton and served as her alternate.

Chapter 17

Advocate for Independent Living

Preparation

God granted me the desire of my heart in May 2004 when I was hired as an advocacy specialist by the Coalition for Independent Living Options, Inc. (CILO) in Stuart, Florida. Twenty-three years earlier, I was introduced to the independent living movement when visiting the Center for Independent Living (CIL) in Berkeley, California—the first CIL in the United States—and the model for roughly 400 CILs nationwide.[1] I had served as a CIL board member in Euclid, Ohio, and a CIL advisory board member in Rochester, New York, and now I was ecstatic to serve as an employee.

Only in hindsight could I see how—all through the years—God had prepared me for CIL employment in Florida:

- As a dwarf, I lived the disability experience, and—for as long as I can remember—advocated for my own acceptance as an equal contributing member of society.

- I had law degrees in New Zealand and Maryland and admission to the bar in New Zealand, Ohio, and New York.

- As a lawyer in New Zealand, I advocated for clients in civil and criminal courts.

- As a project editor for Lawyers Cooperative Publishing (now known as Thomson Reuters), I wrote disability civil rights law books for lawyers.

- As an LPA volunteer, I was a leader in banning dwarf tossing in licensed establishments in New York and Florida, and breaking the six-inch reach barrier in buildings and facilities open to the public throughout America.

- As a staff writer for the Christian Law Association, I wrote religious liberty articles and training materials for nonlawyers.

Outreach and Networking

Although well prepared to work as an advocacy specialist, I was still in new territory as the first and only CILO advocate assigned to a new office covering three Treasure Coast counties. As a result, outreach and networking were needed to make CILO services known in the community. It helped that our office shared space with the One Stop Career Center—now known as CareerSource Research Coast—because I received many referrals from One Stop staff and other agencies under their roof. Membership in the Martin County Interagency Coalition also gave me a forum for promoting CILO services.

Community education on advocacy was also important. Clearly, advocating on all disability issues in three counties was impossible for one person. The best way for me to increase my impact was to teach advocacy principles so that others could not only speak for themselves as self-advocates, but also speak for someone else as an individual advocate, and make change for others as system advocates. From half-hour to all-day classes, I gave advocacy training to people with a variety of mental and physical disabilities, parents of children with disabilities, and professionals providing home- and community-based Medwaiver[2] or special education services.

Emergency Operations

Hurricanes Frances and Jeanne in September 2004, and Wilma in October 2005, solved my quandary of what advocacy issue to tackle first. CILO services were definitely needed in the Martin Interagency Network on Disabilities (MIND). I attended regular MIND meetings to address the needs of those who didn't have the means to prepare for, or recover from, the devastating storms. About the same time, I joined a Florida Department of Health Disability Task Force that provided funding for several conferences on emergency preparedness for people with disabilities. In 2007, I coordinated one of these conferences in Martin County in collaboration with nine nonprofit and government agencies.[3]

The Martin County conference lived up to expectations with a keynote address by Mike Lyons, a severe-weather expert and meteorologist for the ABC TV channel WPBF 25. Mike was both a drawing card for attendance and a hit with attendees. There was audience participation following each panel on legislation, preparation and notification, and response and recovery. Personal responsibility was emphasized, and professionals increased their understanding of the needs of people with disabilities.

A media article reporting on the conference covered key unresolved issues, such as alerting residents with hearing and vision impairments of the need to evacuate. Hugh Curran, past president of Deaf and Hard of Hearing Services (DHHS) of the Treasure Coast, told how people who are deaf were knocking on the door of his home during the eye of

Hurricane Frances because they couldn't hear the radio reports and thought the storm was over.

Keith Holman, the director of Martin County Emergency Management, lamented that his agency, "can't afford to have hurricane guides printed in Braille [. . .] We barely have them in Spanish."

Angela stands and speaks holding a microphone in her left hand and a notepad in her right hand as she makes an announcement at the Martin county conference on emergency preparedness for people with disabilities. Keith Holman, seated at a table behind her, looks down at the papers in front of him.

As hoped, the conference was the beginning and not the end of addressing emergency-preparedness issues for people with disabilities in the county. Indeed, the conference was the impetus for forming the Martin County task force on Emergency Preparedness for People with Disabilities (EPD). For several years, the EPD task force met quarterly to address emergency notifications and emergency shelters

concerns: accessible cots, pets, service animals, pre-regis-
tration, volunteer sensitivity training, and transportation.

Lamentably, the influence of the EPD task force dimin-
ished as local disasters faded in the rearview mirror, agency personnel and priorities changed, and meetings became
less frequent. This was obvious when Hurricane Irma hit in
September 2017. I was appalled when there was no American Sign Language (ASL) interpreter at Emergency Management televised announcements. I joined with Rick Kottler,
executive director of DHHS of the Treasure Coast, to send a
letter to the Martin County administrator:

> *It is imperative that these broadcasts are*
> *accessible to all county residents! [. . .] The*
> *ASL interpreter needs to agree to stay housed*
> *at the Emergency Operations Center during*
> *the emergency event. As many other counties*
> *found out, finding an interpreter at the last*
> *minute does not work. Or in the case of Man-*
> *atee County, they hired an inept interpreter,*
> *and the community is in an uproar.*

The county administrator admitted the weakness and
agreed that it is critical for the county to effectively message
all residents during a disaster.

Voting Rights

Another advocacy priority soon emerged—voting rights.
Among other things, the Help America Vote Act of 2002
required that voting facilities and equipment be accessible
to people with disabilities. The training of election officials,
poll workers, and volunteers was mandated to promote participation of individuals with disabilities.

The Martin County Supervisor of Elections diligently held elections in accessible facilities and purchased accessible equipment. Moreover, she turned to CILO to train election workers on disability sensitivity. In the 2006 election, I did face-to-face trainings in multiple sessions. In the 2008 election, I was among those taped for an online video class. In these trainings, I taught that people with disabilities—

— expect equal treatment—not pity, paternalism, or a pedestal.

— shouldn't be described by their disability.

— value independence, meaning that they will ask for help if it's needed and direct how requested help should be given.

— need the same space and privacy given to other voters.

— shouldn't be asked if they are disabled because disclosure is only required if a reasonable accommodation is requested.

During and after my tenure with CILO, I continued to support elections staff with disability sensitivity training. I also demonstrated the inclusion of people with disabilities in the election process by serving as a poll worker from 2012 through 2018. To make it through the 14-hour day, I needed two accommodations: (1) a block of wood placed under the back legs of my assigned Electronic Voting Identification Device to tilt it forward so that I could see the screen and reach the voter pass printout; and (2) a custom Ergo Chair with adjustable height, a modified seat, and an attached footrest that raises and lowers with the chair.[4]

Fair Housing Access

My legal training prepared me to push back against home-owner association (HOA) discriminatory practices against residents with disabilities. Threatened with daily fines for violation of HOA rules, people with various physical disabilities came to me for help. I advocated for their right to an equal opportunity to use and enjoy their homes with reasonable accommodations as provided in federal law—the Fair Housing Amendments Act of 1988. I would meet with the distraught HOA resident in their community, assess their situation, read management correspondence and rules, and respond to management with either a letter or face-to-face meeting.

Many of these consumers had resided in their communities for several years without incident. The hostility towards them arose when new and inflexible management enacted new rules as shown in the situations below:

- *Shirley* had parking violation notices placed on her SUV parked close to the entrance of the building where she lived. Her mobility impairment made it impossible for her to walk to the distant newly designated area for SUVs. Despite having a disabled parking permit, the HOA was considering its right to tow her SUV, boot it, or impose a daily fine. My letter on *Shirley*'s behalf persuaded management that federal law trumps HOA parking rules.

- *Margaret's* HOA directed her to move the pavers off her lawn to maintain the uniform appearance in front of the parking spaces. *Margaret* needed the pavers to provide a solid walking surface as a shortcut to her vehicle. *Margaret* was unable to walk the long way around on the sidewalk next to the building. The HOA manager's bravado disintegrated when I met him in person. Even he could see his rationale for the paver rule should succumb to *Margaret*'s need for the paver accommodation.

- *Joyce* parked her battery-powered scooter on the walkway outside her unit when charging it. Her neighbor complained about the obstruction to the path of travel. I proposed two alternatives: (1) install an electrical outlet under the stairwell so that the scooter could be charged without being parked on the walkway; or (2) widen the sidewalk in front of *Joyce*'s unit to allow a three-foot clear path of travel. Neither option was necessary when the neighbor stopped her seasonal visits.

- Mike Youngblood took his service dog, Hannah, off-leash for her daily exercise run. Management objected to this violation of the HOA off-leash rule and posted a No Pet sign on the vacant lots where Hannah exercised. Mike is an amputee, has epilepsy, and uses a power wheelchair for mobility. Hannah is not a pet and is individually trained to fetch what Mike drops and to run for help should he fall or have a seizure. Hannah is obedient to 30 voice commands and doesn't need a leash to stay close to Mike. After I exchanged letters with the HOA attorney, Mike was granted a reasonable accommodation allowing Hannah to run off-leash.

None of the accommodations listed above cost the HOA any money, unlike *Marilyn*'s case. *Marilyn* was able

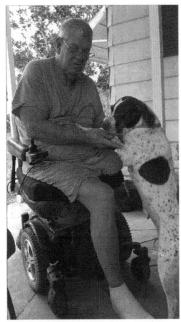

Mike seated in his power wheelchair shows one foot touching the ground and his short leg amputated above the knee. Hannah, Mike's service dog, stands with her back legs on the ground as Mike looks down at her and cradles her front leg resting on his chest.

to use the security key to unlock the front door of her apartment building, but she ambulated so slowly with her walker that the lock clicked closed before she reached the door. Besides, even if *Marilyn* reached the door before it locked, she was too weak to pull open the heavy door. The HOA was persuaded to purchase and install an electronic door opener.

Financial Assistance Awards

In cases where home modifications were not the responsibility of the HOA, CILO could often provide financial assistance to consumers who met the criteria. Among the Treasure Coast home modifications that I approved funding for were portable and permanent ramps, grab bars in showers, roll-in showers replacing bathtubs, accessible plumbing fixtures, widened doorways and lowered countertops for wheelchair access, a stairlift, and handrails on stairs.

The funding for these home modifications was made possible by the Treasure Coast Fund that was fed by donations, fundraising, fee awards from winning Social Security cases, and class action settlement awards shared with Florida CILs. Our first and largest donation came from a Martin

County Commission candidate impressed by CILO's June 17, 2008, public transit demonstration at the Martin Board of County Commissioners (BOCC). The candidate told me on the day of the demonstration that if he wasn't elected, he would donate what remained in his campaign fund to CILO. When he lost the election, I was impressed that he remembered saying this and donated a little over $2,000. Funds went even further when we shared expenses in partnership with an individual's GoFundMe campaign or agencies, such as the Brain and Spinal Cord Injury Program, the Council on Aging, the Veterans Administration, or the Florida Division of Vocational Rehabilitation.

Treasure Coast Fund awards were also approved for a battery charger, batteries for power wheelchairs and scooters, wheelchair repairs, a trailer hitch for a wheelchair lift, a wheelchair stander, an electric Hoyer lift, an assisted-lift recliner, and a hospital bed.

The opening of the Treasure Coast Equipment Lending Closet in 2008—managed by staff members I supervised—also made it possible for CILO to give away donated equipment that met home access and mobility needs, such as bath, toilet, and stairlift chairs; and walkers, wheelchairs, and scooters.

Chapter 18

Transit Funding and Public Participation

Call to Action

While working as a CILO advocate, I saw the need for advocacy to fund transportation systems. A crisis exploded after transit funding for FY2008 (fiscal year) took a 31% cut in state and federal funding. The cuts forced a reduction from 27 to 18 transit routes in Martin County where I worked. When the county proposed an additional 20% in budget cuts in FY2009, a call to action was imperative.

I recruited, trained, and organized transit riders to plead with the Martin BOCC not to cut public transit funds. As someone who had been driving since age 18, I wasn't the most critical person to speak. More important spokespeople were those directly affected by the cuts—those unable to drive due to brain injuries, cognitive limitations, epilepsy, the effect of prescribed medications, vision loss, and a myriad of other physical and mental impairments. Commissioners had to know how lives would be impacted if riders couldn't take the bus to medical appointments, work, college, and stores. Any further reduction in public transit would result in medical emergencies, unemployment, and malnutrition.

I trained riders dependent on public transit to confront commissioners with emails, letters, one-on-one meetings, personal impact statements, and public comments at weekly BOCC televised meetings. One rider received an ovation in the BOCC chamber after sharing her experience about a trip denial to a medical office. She had to ride her bike seven miles in a heat index of 107°F. She was late to the appointment and took 20 minutes to recover. Worse yet were the many who—after being denied a bus ride—were unable to compensate by riding a bike.

Several media reports put the spotlight on 17 Community Coach public transit riders and advocates picketing at the Martin County Administrative Center on June 17, 2008.[1] The picketers were blind or visually impaired, brain injured, mentally ill, and wheelchair users carrying hand-made pickets that read:

- MARTIN NEEDS COACH

- SAVE THE COACH, SAVE JOBS

- LET ME RIDE

- COACH IS MY LIFELINE

- COACH IS CRITICAL

- FULLY FUND COACH

- NO COACH NO ALTERNATIVE

- NO COACH NO WAY OUT

Three of the five commissioners responded to my request that they talk to individual picketers during a break from the BOCC meeting. The commissioners responded favorably to the demonstration and went on the record assuring riders that funding for the bus service would remain. Two commissioners agreed that cutting bus funding would threaten the jobs of both riders and bus drivers.

Despite the warm reception at the June BOCC demonstration, riders continued advocacy at the July budget workshop to be sure the commissioners didn't renege on their agreement to spare transit from county budget cuts. And the commissioners were true to their word. Indeed, public transit funding for FY2009 increased 13%.[2]

The successful transportation advocacy experience in 2008 set the standard for my next ten years at CILO. I didn't organize another demonstration, but each year I read the proposed county budget to determine whether to support or oppose it. In addition to making my own public comments, I recruited and trained riders to give public comments at the annual Martin BOCC budget workshop. I also met individually with all five county commissioners prior to the workshop.

ADA Violations of Public Participation

In January 2012, a new public transit issue emerged when the Martin BOCC introduced a fixed-route system with a complementary ADA Paratransit Plan—door-to-door service for those unable to ride fixed-route buses. In my role as a CILO advocate, I recognized that county staff sought BOCC approval of the plan without giving adequate notice or opportunity for the public participation required by federal law.

After receiving a reliable tip of the county staff's intention to circumvent ADA requirements, I recruited public transit riders to join me in making public comments to ask the Martin BOCC to postpone approval of the paratransit plan. Staff had failed to reach out to potential paratransit riders or people with disabilities and groups representing them in the community.

Notice of the public hearing was grossly inadequate. The public notice of the proposed plan had been posted in *a* newspaper, but not in *the* newspaper read by the WQCS Radio Reading Service for approximately 500 blind or visually-impaired listeners. And no notices were posted on public transit buses or distributed to organizations whose clients used public transit.

Our advocacy achieved the desired result when the Martin BOCC declined to adopt the ADA Paratransit Plan and directed staff to come back after working out the notice and public participation issues with me. After five years of advocating in support of public transit funding—including my annual appointments with individual commissioners—the entire BOCC knew me by name. The chair of the BOCC declared me trustworthy and listened to me instead of county staff.

Although county staff also knew me, they weren't so appreciative. The staff member who had prepared and presented the ADA Paratransit Plan cried when the BOCC declined to adopt the plan. Still, she had no choice but to work with me. After following my lead on how to give adequate notice and meaningful outreach to the disability community, public participation on the plan was scheduled in March 2012. Even so, county staff still saw this as "Angela's" meeting that would only need a small conference room. When 30 people turned up, staff had to open the county commission chamber at the last minute.

Staff were astounded that 15 people made public comments—nine riders, five disability professionals, and one employer—giving meaningful input on the plan.[3] Staff listened to the public input and responded with many improvements to the plan relating to eligibility recertification, the trip pick-up window, consideration of weather conditions that affect a person's ability to get to a bus stop, and the appeal process. Finally, I was ready to support the revised ADA Paratransit Plan when staff resubmitted it to the Martin BOCC in July 2012.

Another recurring issue was the Martin Metropolitan Planning Organization's scheduling of public participation transit workshops on evening and weekend hours when there was no transit service. This precluded public transit and transportation disadvantaged (TD) riders from giving input into the county's ten-year Transit Development Plan and 2035 Regional Long Range Public Transportation Plan. Staff advice that people with disabilities could give input via emails or the phone were separate and unequal alternatives. As a result, in 2013, I guided the new citizen-advocate rider member of the Martin Local Coordinating Board (LCB) on how to make a motion for consideration by the LCB. She was a quick study and immediately moved that public workshops be scheduled at times when TD riders could get there either by providing after-hours transit or scheduling daytime meetings. The motion passed unanimously.

Transportation Disadvantaged (TD)

My foray into public transportation advocacy as a CILO advocate also led to my discovery of the Martin County Transportation Disadvantaged Local Coordinating Board (TD LCB). This was one of Florida's 67 county boards managed by the Florida Commission for the Transportation Disadvantaged (CTD) which had been established by the Florida legislature in 1989.[4] The CTD administered the funding allocated by the state for transportation services for older adults, persons with disabilities, persons of low income, and children at risk.

Soon after I began attending Martin TD LCB meetings in 2007 and asking questions during the public comment period, I was appointed as one of the 18 LCB members. Each member represents a particular agency or population; I represented the Florida Association for Community Action, an organization that serves those who are economically disadvantaged.

I served as an LCB member for eleven years. In this role, I participated in quarterly and annual meetings that, among other things, involved the Community Transportation Coordinator (CTC) selection, monthly performance reports and annual evaluations; trip reimbursement rates; and developing the five-year Transportation Disadvantaged Service Plan (TDSP) with annual updates. For several years, I contributed to the CTC annual evaluation by surveying transit contractors and riders and traveling in vehicles with riders. This helped me see how important the TD system was to riders. For example, the final question on the rider survey was, "What does transportation mean to you?" Typical answers included:

- It is the only way to get to my appointments.

- It gives me freedom to get around.

- They get me to the doctor on time and make sure I get home.

- I can't get to dialysis without it.

- I love it, great people, don't treat me like a patient.

- I get to keep on living.

- Everything.

I had input into the writing of two five-year plans in Martin County. For example, I successfully advocated to remove the service-animal restrictions that were in violation of the ADA and to add education in the list of trip priorities, namely: medical, education, employment, grocery shopping/nutrition, social service agencies, and other social/shopping/life-sustaining activities.

Although not a member of the Saint Lucie County (SLC) TD LCB, in 2018 I advocated with *Pamela*—a SLC resident—to add employment as a priority trip in the SLC TDSP. Blindness prevented *Pamela* from driving and, for two decades, she commuted to her part-time job using the TD program with a one-dollar co-pay each way. When *Pamela* moved to more affordable housing, she didn't know there was no TD bus route to her job from her new residence. Although the county switched *Pamela* to a grant-funded transit program, she couldn't afford the 20% co-pays for each trip.

I successfully advocated to save *Pamela*'s job in the short term when CILO, the Division of Blind Services, and the county partnered to cover the co-pays. The long-term solution involved me organizing *Pamela*, other riders with disabilities, and agencies to speak at the SLC TD LCB quarterly meeting. *Pamela* was among the speakers informing the LCB of the huge need to make work trips a priority.

Chapter 19

Social Security Benefits Representation

On the Job Training

When I came to CILO, I only had rudimentary knowledge of the Social Security benefits law. This proved to be insufficient for the children and adults with disabilities in great need of help navigating the bureaucracy of the Social Security Administration (SSA). My first inclination was to refer these cases to attorneys, but I discovered that attorneys are selective about which cases they take—which leaves many people without representation.

When *Jose* presented me with an SSA letter denying his benefits claim despite his inability to continue working in construction after two heart attacks, I decided to dig in and teach myself Social Security law. *Jose* was in total despair believing the SSA was waiting for him to die. The insufficiency of my sympathetic ear motivated me to acquire the knowledge needed to help the next claimant the SSA sent into a downward spiral.

My self-training was both academic and practical. I researched the law, attended seminars, and trained on-the-job helping claimants with applications and appeals, as well as SSA overpayments and reporting requirements.

Appointed Representative

It astounded me that the SSA didn't require appointed representatives to be licensed attorneys. This meant I could represent claimants in appeal hearings before administrative law judges (ALJs) without admission to the Florida bar. As an appointed representative, I could access secure SSA electronic files, speak on behalf of the claimant, submit and receive SSA documents, and receive fees when the claim was successful.

Because not all SSA cases are winners, I had to use good judgment in accepting or declining which claimants to represent. Although CILO didn't have the financial pressure of needing to win cases to stay in business, there was pressure not to waste my limited resources on losing cases. I was spread very thin covering multiple disability issues with no secretarial or paralegal support. Time spent on SSA cases needed to be meaningful.

I was up against the wall in the case of *Jade*, a teenager with a full-scale intelligence quotient (FSIQ) of 61. Her mother spoke minimal English, and there were no funds to pay for a Spanish interpreter. A solution immediately came to mind in the person of *Jorge*, who had benefited from transportation advocacy and given me a standing offer to help in any way he could. With Spanish as his first language, he was more than willing to interpret for Spanish-speaking consumers with limited English.

Even so, *Jorge's* help involved some creativity. *Jorge* was transportation-disadvantaged, and coming to my office for this purpose wasn't a prioritized trip. Using technology to our advantage, *Jorge* called into the office from his home and interpreted via the speaker phone as I prepared an eight-page SSA form with *Jade* and her mother.

Another way of stretching resources was to partner with

claimants. For example, I often asked them to request and pick up copies of their own medical records.

The Medical Record

The key to winning an SSA case is developing a record with evidence that shows the claimant is unable to work because of a medical condition that is expected to last at least 12 months or result in death. This does not mean unable to do any work, but rather unable to do substantial gainful activity (SGA) which is work that pays more than a designated dollar amount per month.[1]

Building a medical record is a huge challenge when the claimant's loss of employment also results in loss of health insurance and access to health care. In these cases, claimants must rely on the willingness and ability of friends or family to pay medical expenses, free or subsidized medical clinics willing to run tests and complete SSA paperwork, and programs like Partnership for Prescription Assistance to pay for necessary medications. As a last resort, claimants can request a medical examination by a physician contracted by the SSA. For the most part, SSA exams are limited and the conclusions lean heavily in favor of the government.

Appeals

More than two-thirds of SSA disability benefit initial claims are denied. This results in hardship and confusion for those who have a good case. However, after I reviewed the record on which many initial decisions were based, I could see that claimants often answered questions poorly. Sometimes claimants misunderstood the purpose of the questions and answered as if applying for a job. Rather than reporting how the limitations of their disability negatively impacted their ability to work, they highlighted accomplishments believing this would persuade the SSA that they deserved a benefit.

A Request for Reconsideration (first appeal) can be filed for those whose initial claims are denied. Yet the wait time for an answer can be another eight months or so during which time the record can be updated with new information. Here again, everything depends on the written record since the claimant does not meet with the one making the decision. This is a good thing for claimants who are poor witnesses.

For instance, I was relieved when *Crystal*—a physical and emotional wreck—won her appeal on reconsideration and didn't have to testify. *Crystal* had continued to work as a legal secretary despite experiencing depression and anxiety, two motor vehicle accidents, and domestic violence. She was finally broken and lost her job after a boat accident caused a painful spinal injury. As if that wasn't enough, she was then diagnosed with fibromyalgia and reflex sympathetic dystrophy syndrome.

An ALJ hearing (second appeal) can be requested if the Request for Reconsideration is denied. Although getting a hearing date is typically about two years after the initial application, it's the first time the claimant is face-to-face with a judge either in person or via a video conference call.

Many claimants are tempted to give up before they get a hearing. They file a new claim and once again are denied by those who base their decision on the paperwork. Claimants who receive a denial letter are much better off pursuing their appeal options. Waiting for an ALJ hearing greatly improves the likelihood of receiving a favorable decision.

Continuing a Child's SSI After Turning 18

Claimants who have received SSI as children are reevaluated

at age 18 to determine if they meet the disability criteria for adults. In building the record in these 18-year-old redetermination cases, I solicited input from Exceptional Student Education (ESE) teachers and job consultants exploring claimant employment options. In the case of *Amber*—who had a FSIQ of about 63 and marked difficulties in daily living activities—I asked her job-training ESE teacher to complete an SSA teacher questionnaire. I was mystified when the teacher rated *Amber*'s performance very favorably.

I went back to the teacher and asked, "If *Amber* did so well as an intern, why did she not get hired by the employer like other successful interns?"

The teacher realized she had rated *Amber*'s effort—not her abilities—and redid the questionnaire to accurately reflect her employment limitations.

Not long before *Amber*'s ALJ hearing, she began working part-time in a supported employment position cleaning roadside rest area bathrooms. Now I had to explain to the ALJ why *Amber* could work part-time, but not full-time. For this, I depended on her supervisor's assessment who reported the following:

> *About two weeks into the job, Amber was unable to complete her normal routine during an eight-hour shift. When asked why, she said she was too tired to finish everything. As she said this, she became very emotional and started to cry. This was her third day in a row, working eight hours each day. We are currently short on help and I would love to let Amber work 32 hours per week instead of 24. However, I do not believe Amber would be able to work more than 24 hours per week.*

The ALJ was satisfied with this explanation and congratulated *Amber* for having a job and her parents for encouraging this. After checking with me that *Amber*'s earnings were below the SGA level, the ALJ made a favorable decision on *Amber*'s appeal.

Another reason for the SSA to continue the SSI benefit for beneficiaries after they turn 18 is that they are still participating in an individual education plan (IEP) for an individual aged 18 through 21.[2] For example, *Kyle's* SSI was continued for two additional years to allow him time to complete his high school graduation requirements under his IEP. Given this opportunity, *Kyle* went on to gainful employment as an adult and no longer needed SSI. *Kyle* eventually became the manager of a fast food restaurant.

Winning and Losing

If approved for SSA benefits, in addition to a monthly payment, the claimant may receive a lump sum payment in past due benefits. Because *Donald's* case dragged on for five years, he received over $100,000 and CILO earned the full $6,000 representative fee. *Donald* was overwhelmed. We worked hard for this favorable finding, but there was definitely some Divine intervention on the outcome.

For about ten years, I successfully represented many claimants in ALJ hearings before many different judges. The disabilities—individually or in combination—ranged from ADHD, anxiety and depression, blindness, blood clots, cancer and lymphedema, diabetes, epilepsy, intellectual, learning, migraines, neurological, neuromuscular, orthopedic, and strokes. Yet despite my best efforts, not all cases had favorable outcomes.

Often the losing cases were in the gray zone and depended on the claimant's credibility as to pain levels and incapacity. Occasionally I even agreed with an ALJ's ruling that a claimant wasn't credible. For example, over time I learned that *Nicole* lied to me about taking her epilepsy medication. This was proven by her blood work and doctor's notes in the patient's file saying that *Nicole* was noncompliant with her medication. This caused me to question *Nicole*'s credibility on how much pain she had from a back injury. But when an ALJ rejected the claims of people I believed to be very credible, I feared for their future without income from a job or a disability benefit.

SSA Overpayments

SSA overpayment cases were stressful for beneficiaries and time-consuming for me. In the course of one year, *Linda* received several letters from the SSA claiming that she had been overpaid amounts ranging from $9,425 to $18,586. The SSA didn't explain why the amount for which they claimed repayment kept increasing. *Linda* was on the verge of a breakdown when SSA sent a letter saying that she wouldn't receive any benefit payment the next month. *Linda* had lost one home to Hurricane Frances—she didn't want to lose her current home to a mortgage foreclosure. *Sharon*, another beneficiary with insurmountable overpayment SSA letters, was suicidal.

I worked with both *Linda* and *Sharon*—and other beneficiaries—trying to piece together records that might account for the overpayments that racked up when they temporarily returned to work and the SSA continued to make benefit payments. The SSA is notorious for waiting years before sending overpayment letters. In the meantime, the benefit amounts received were spent and records were lost. After spending time with some of these beneficiaries, I found that locating copies of letters—the ones beneficiaries said they sent the SSA reporting the times they returned to work—was a lost cause.

I typically settled on a practical solution and made Requests for Waiver of Overpayment Recovery or a Change in the Repayment Rate. An SSA-contracted benefits consultant was skeptical about the SSA's willingness to reduce the monthly repayment amount any lower than $75 a month. He marveled when I negotiated $50 per month withholding for *Linda* and $25 for *Sharon*.

Chapter 20

Special Education for Students with Disabilities

Education Right

The educational landscape for American children with disabilities has changed dramatically over the last 45 years. In 1975, one million of these children were entirely excluded from the public school system, and more than half only had limited access to the education system.[1] Yet, by 2020, almost seven million received special education services.[2] *So what accounts for the drastic change?* The answer lies in the Education for All Handicapped Children Act of 1975[3]—renamed the Individuals with Disabilities Education Act in 1990 (IDEA)[4]—which gave children with disabilities the right to receive a free and appropriate public education in the least restrictive environment based on their individualized needs.

The words sound simple enough but decades after passage of the IDEA, children often need advocates to secure their education rights. My position with CILO gave me the opportunity to step into the education advocate role in Individual Education Plan (IEP) meetings where a student's individual education needs were debated and documented.

Parent Invitation a Prerequisite

The IEP process is often overwhelming for parents who enter a crowded meeting room where as many as 12 school district professionals[5] appear to talk another language and be in cahoots with one another.

As one parent said, "I am so emotionally involved that I often get befuddled when talking about my son in a meeting, and therefore don't express myself or advocate for him the way I need to."

As much as I was ready to deliver advocacy services, I couldn't attend an IEP meeting without a parent's invitation. Even so, invitations were accepted with the understanding that I speak for the student—not the parent. For the most part, parent and child interests aligned, but occasionally I had to go against a parent's wishes. Of course when this happened, I wouldn't be invited to the next meeting.

My initial challenge was letting parents know I was available to attend meetings. My first introduction to parents came from school district staff writing IEPs for high school students transitioning to college, vocational training, job placement, or adult day programs. With parental consent for my presence at the IEP meeting, I shared information on community resources, government programs, and disability issues related to turning 18.

Parent invitations to IEP meetings began flowing after we met at Exceptional Student Education (ESE) Parent Advisory Council meetings, Project Connect, Treasure Coast Interagency Transition Council events, and parent support groups. Word of mouth soon resulted in my receiving more invitations than I could accept. Therefore, I encouraged parents to check with me before accepting a meeting date to allow for negotiation with the school for a date when I could attend. If this didn't work out, I coached parents on the phone and via email before and after the IEP meeting.

Eligibility for Services

Identifying a student as being eligible for ESE services was a primary issue causing parents to seek advocacy help. Although school districts have a "child find" duty to identify students with disabilities, parents often noticed learning problems long before the school district. This led many parents to pay hundreds of dollars on private psychological or neurological evaluations to identify a disability that would qualify their child for ESE services. Other parents met with resistance when they asked the school for a psychological educational evaluation at school district expense. Some parents got the school district evaluation but disagreed with the result that found no eligibility. In these situations, I held schools accountable to comply with IDEA and end their delay and denial tactics.

One prominent delaying tactic prompted me to give public comment before the Martin County School Board. I answered a school district administrator's favorable report on the Response to Intervention (RTI) program designed to help students struggling with academics.

I commented that a misuse of RTI was delaying identification of students eligible for ESE services, saying: "Any reduction in referrals [to ESE] [. . .] is something to be investigated, not touted as a success."

Late identification of a disability caused irreparable harm to students. This was the case for one student whose learning disability wasn't identified until his senior year in high school when his grade point average was too low to qualify for a graduation diploma.

Sometimes a late identification wasn't a deliberate tactic, but rather a system failure. This was evident in the case of *Justin* who acquired a traumatic brain injury in a skateboarding accident when he was in middle school. After sev-

Angela Van Etten stands with her hand on a chair frame and Tyler Melton crouches next to her with his hand on her shoulder at his high school graduation party. She had been on his IEP team since third grade.

eral days in ICU and several months with Hospital Home-bound instruction, *Justin* finally returned to school. Yet two years of erratic grades, many behavior referrals, and parent pleas for help failed to get the school district's attention.

Nothing changed until a meeting was called in *Justin's* second semester in high school to decide if he should be expelled and sent to an alternate school with juvenile delinquents. This is when his private mental health counselor referred his parents to me. Finally, with education advocacy, the school district conducted a psychological educational evaluation and an IEP team found that *Justin*'s brain injury qualified him for an IEP.

Other eligibility battles involved parents seeking to upgrade their child from a 504 Plan under the Rehabilitation Act to an IEP under the IDEA. With a 504 Plan, a student with a disability qualified for accommodations, but not the specialized instruction that comes with an IEP. For example, students with health-related rather than learning issues were accommodated with things such as extra time for assignments or tests, excused time to take medication or a break, a pass to use the bathroom more often, leaving class early so as not to get caught in the hallway crush, or a key to the elevator. An IEP was not needed. The determination of which plan was appropriate often required intense advocacy in multiple meetings.

One tip-off that a 504 Plan was inadequate and an IEP was more appropriate was when a student's behavior triggered a meeting to determine if the behavior was a manifestation of the disability. This happened when *Alex* entered high school with the 504 Plan he had since third grade due to his impulsivity and disorganization stemming from ADHD. However, when *Alex* accumulated 30 referrals for inappropriate comments and noncompliance with teacher directives, the school pushed to transfer him to an alternative school for students with disciplinary problems. Because the IEP team decided that his behavior was a manifestation of his disability, a psychological educational evaluation was conducted and provided the basis for his team to find *Alex* eligible for an IEP and the ESE supports he needed to manage his behavior. As a result, the school's plan to transfer out this "problem" student failed. *Alex* remained in school with his peers. And with ESE support, he turned his behavior around.

IEP Development and Content

IEPs are developed in a team meeting, must be updated annually, and may be amended during the school year. For the annual IEP update, I recommended that parents request a pre-meeting IEP draft. Even if this draft was received the night before the IEP meeting—which was quite common—parent and advocacy input was more thoughtful, and the meeting time used more efficiently.

I often requested edits to IEP goals and objectives to ensure they met the student's educational needs and were measurable. Some staff resented this kind of scrutiny, but there was no other way to assess whether the student was making the meaningful progress required by IDEA.

Other staff were more receptive, as indicated by one ESE team leader who said: "When I am writing something in an IEP, I often think, 'What would Angela Van Etten say about this?' And then I smile, and make sure it is in clear and understandable language so there is no confusion."

Some students regress during the IEP year. Such was the case for *Chris* who for successive years suffered from unstable staffing of his ESE classroom. The IEP team has no control over absenteeism of teachers caused by death, medical issues, administrative removal pending the outcome of a criminal charge, and a revolving door of substitute teachers.

In addition to measurable goals, I advocated for the student's need for services, such as occupational therapy, physical therapy, speech and language therapy, mental health counseling, or special transportation. The needs of each student were individualized as shown in the following two special transportation cases.

For *Victoria*, a high school student who is blind, I successfully advocated to remove the special transportation coding from her IEP. *Victoria* was devastated when the regular bus driver told her she must ride the special bus with an aide. *Victoria's* orientation and mobility training equipped her to ride the regular school bus with her peers—supervision from an aide was insulting.

Chris is all smiles as he exits his house in a light blue striped shirt ready for the best part of his day—riding the school bus.

In contrast, for *Chris*, a middle school student who is high needs on the autism spectrum, I successfully advocated for his IEP to add special training for bus drivers and bus aides. The need for training was evident when *Chris* became the victim of a bus aide who grabbed him to stop him getting off the bus upon arrival at his school when nobody was waiting to meet him.

Chris can't tolerate being touched and swung his arm back against the bus aide in self-defense. The aide fought back by filing criminal assault charges against *Chris* even though he doesn't have the mental capacity to form intent. It took a special meeting with the school district attorney and high-level administration officials to agree on bus procedures to keep both staff and *Chris* safe. The criminal charges against *Chris*

were eventually dropped, but not until after his parents paid
a hefty retainer to a criminal defense attorney.

Another important element in an IEP is the listing of accommodations the student with a disability needs to level
the playing field with regular education students. Typically,
this list was easily developed with teachers willing to check
off what the student needed to be successful. The frustration
came when delivery of IEP accommodations wasn't timely.
For example, *Victoria* and *Nicholas*—two middle school students who were blind—needed my advocacy in multiple IEP
meetings to get:

(1) teacher notes, study guides, and work corrections at
    the same time as other students;
(2) current and functional technology and software so
    that they could work with other students and print
    work for the teacher; and
(3) independence from adults through peer supports.

Placement

A frequent area of contention in developing an IEP is de-
termining the least restrictive environment or placement.
Hospital Homebound is the most restrictive environment
with only one teacher, one student, and no opportunity for
interaction with other students. As a result, the criteria are
strict—dependent on medical evidence—and intended to
be short term. Over the years, I advocated for students in
Hospital Homebound who had muscular dystrophy, mental
health diagnoses, cancer, and autism. The students' needs
varied from being inappropriately placed, seeking to extend
their stay, or wanting to come to school for an occasional
social event.

For an ESE student able to attend school, the IEP team
decides what percentage of the day the student will spend in

an ESE class, regular class, or combination of the two. I cut my advocacy teeth in two intense battles for inclusion in regular classes on behalf of *Anthony* and *Sarah*. Both students had intellectual impairments and were in self-contained ESE second grade classes at different schools. Staff considered it cruel to place *Anthony* and *Sarah* with their same-age peers in regular education classes where they might be teased and frustrated with academic expectations. One school district program specialist was so emotional in her opposition that genuine tears streamed down her face.

In the case of *Sarah*, the IEP team reluctantly agreed to a six-week trial in which data would be collected on meeting classroom expectations—staying in her seat, raising her hand, not calling out or being otherwise disruptive—and academic performance in a preferred subject. The data supported incremental increases in *Sarah*'s time spent in regular education classes provided she had support from an ESE teacher. Eventually *Sarah* graduated from high school as a pioneer student mainstreamed in regular education classes while using the modified Access Points curriculum used by students with intellectual disabilities. In the spring concert of her senior year chorus class, *Sarah* received a standing ovation for singing a duet, "I'll Make the Difference."[6]

In the case of *Anthony*, he graduated from high school with his picture hanging in the front lobby with this quotation: "No one succeeds without effort [. . .] Those who succeed owe their success to perseverance."

One key to student success in the mainstream is the specially designed service of support facilitation from an ESE teacher in the regular education classroom. Yet despite this essential support, many IEPs didn't allocate sufficient support even when the IEP team conceded there was a need. Even though the IDEA mandates that IEP services be based on individual needs—not available resources—the schools were stuck with the staffing allocation they received from the school district. This recurring story from multiple schools motivated me to give public comment at a school board meeting highlighting the need to increase the special education budget so that more ESE support facilitation teachers could be allocated to schools.

Change in Placement and Manifestation Meetings

Behavior is a key factor in placement decisions. As a result, I prioritized accepting invitations to manifestation meetings where the student was already suspended, and the IEP team could expel or make a change in placement to a more restrictive environment. If the behavior was unrelated to the disability, then the student would be disciplined under the code applied to students without disabilities. If the behavior was a manifestation of the disability, then the team reviewed the IEP to see if a change in placement was appropriate, or if additional supports were needed.

I often advocated for a behavior analyst to join the IEP team to direct the collection of data used in writing a behavior intervention plan (BIP). This data was used to understand student triggers for the behavior and incentives to extinguish it. The analyst could then use the data to instruct staff how to respond when the behavior occurred. When properly written and followed, a BIP could avoid the need for a change in placement. Such was the case for *Zachary*, a middle school student classified with an emotional and behavioral disorder (EBD).

At 12 years old, *Zachary* was at risk for being pulled from his regular education class and placed in a separate EBD unit at a different school due to his multiple suspensions and detentions, not turning in assignments, and refusal to do classwork. Changes in his IEP and BIP led to his improved behavior. *Zachary* responded positively to counseling, was removed from his physical education class—where many conflicts occurred—and was issued a safe pass to leave class when he was overwhelmed.

Even so, a year later *Zachary* hit a bump in the road, subjecting him to the criminal justice system. He pulled the fire alarm, causing the evacuation of 1,000 students and the staff in the adjacent school superintendent's office. As his advocate, I encouraged *Zachary* to tell the truth. His confession was pivotal to *Zachary* receiving a civil citation for a first offense with no criminal record. He was required to apologize, do community service, and honor a curfew. There was no change in placement, given the approaching end of his last year in middle school.

In the case of aggressive behaviors, a safety plan is sometimes needed. *Miguel*, a student with autism, needed a safety plan when his aggression towards staff and students required the classroom to be cleared as often as three times a day. Blocking mats and restraints were used to protect his teacher and others from injury and *Miguel* was suspended. In *Miguel's* case, a medication change resulted in a dramatic improvement in behavior making the safety plan redundant.

Andrew's high agitation, aggression towards staff, and severe self-injurious behaviors weren't so easily resolved by his IEP team. *Andrew* is on the high needs end of the autism spectrum and was in a small and highly structured separate ESE class with a ratio of three students to one adult. This placement was appropriate until *Andrew's* behavior inexplicably changed at age 14. I accepted the invitation to join the IEP team when *Andrew's* father feared a change in placement to an alternative school.

Despite the perseverance of *Andrew's* IEP team—numerous revisions to his BIP, the temporary trial of a half-day schedule and then Hospital Homebound—his behavior didn't improve. The IEP team reluctantly changed *Andrew*'s placement to an alternative school more able to address his severe behaviors. At this school, *Andrew* became a class of one student with three assigned staff. Thankfully, after six months of intensive behavior therapy with input from an expert in behavior analysis and self-injurious behaviors, *Andrew* transitioned into an ESE class with four students and three support staff. At age 16, *Andrew* was calm, content, and settled in the alternative school. And no one was getting hurt.

Prayer was a key element in changing meeting outcomes. *Andrew*'s father flabbergasted everyone with a request to open his son's annual IEP meeting in prayer. Before anyone could say no, he just went ahead and prayed for God's wisdom and guidance during the meeting. As a parent, he was the only one in the room free to do this. I typically prayed silently for meeting outcomes and encouraged people of faith to have others praying as well. I know these prayers made a positive difference.

Fidelity in Following a Plan

Even when appropriate plans are in place, vigilance is required to ensure plans are followed. Usually, the failure to follow a plan becomes evident when something goes wrong. In the case of *John*, he was suspended and facing expulsion for a zero-tolerance drug offense. He had gone for a walk with some students during the lunch hour and was caught in an off-limits zone where his peers smoked pot and left him to take the rap for holding the foil they passed to him.

John's IEP eligibility was based on "other health impaired" due to his diagnosis of ADHD that, among other things, caused him to seek the attention of his peers and impaired his judgment resulting in bad decisions and a lack of skills needed to escape risky situations. The IEP team agreed that *John*'s behavior was a manifestation of his disability, but only the ESE team leader conceded that the incident was a failure to implement the IEP. *John*'s ESE teacher hadn't provided the weekly specially designed instruction services provided in his IEP. The identification of this and several other breakdowns in ESE services for *John* resulted in a successful appeal to a school district disciplinary committee. *John* was allowed to return to school with a behavior contract and the school's commitment to implement his IEP.

Unfortunately, failure to follow an IEP is not an isolated incident. *Brandon* and *James*, who both had autism, transitioned to middle school with IEPs calling for their placement in regular education classes with ESE support. Even so, staffing issues in regular education classes caused "temporary" placement in the separate ESE autism class. The attempt to place *Brandon* and *James* in one regular education class was abandoned when they were both bullied. Their unlawful placements continued for several months until IEP meetings were finally scheduled and advocacy for appropriate placements was successful.

System Advocacy at School Board Meetings

System advocacy was vital when school district decisions affected multiple ESE students at the same time. For example, in my third week back to work after my aortic valve replacement surgery in 2013, I accepted an invitation to speak at the Supporting Overcoming Understanding Loving (SOUL) parent group for students with autism in anticipation of a relaxed informal question-and-answer session at the end of the school year.

However, it became clear that the parents only had one question on their minds: "Why was a bombshell dropped that our children can't return to our middle school in the next school year?"

One child reported to his parents that he had been kicked out of school because he had done something wrong. A few parents heard on the grapevine that changes were in the wind and only one parent received official word in an IEP meeting that the autism ESE unit was moving to another middle school.

We spent the remainder of the meeting planning for the SOUL parents to share this debacle at the school board meeting the following week. My attendance was more challenging than usual. I was still rebuilding my strength after eight weeks medical leave and the meeting was in rural Indiantown, 20 miles away. I carpooled with parents to save the stress of night driving on country roads. Yet stress was unavoidable when our drive on unfamiliar country roads with poor visibility in the pouring rain was too fast for my liking. Due to unfamiliarity with school layout, the parents and I were dropped off on the wrong side of the campus with a long walk to the correct location. In God's strength, I made it to the meeting room, dried off, and regained my composure before the school board meeting.

As planned at the SOUL meeting, many parents joined me in giving public comments. Those too nervous to speak showed their support by standing as other parents spoke. Our message was clear and simple—communication with parents and students is not a step to be skipped, especially for something as significant as relocating a specialized unit from one school to another. Speaking up was key to ensuring a positive start in the next school year.

Personal Access Barriers and Impact

In my 13 years of ESE advocacy, I advocated for about 1,500 students ages 3-22 in 57 different schools in Martin and Saint Lucie counties. In some of the older school buildings, I had to overcome personal access barriers before I could address any student issues. I encountered entry steps with no railings, curbs with no access ramp, parking too far from the school entrance, out-of-reach doorbells and bathroom door locks, counters and windows above my head that kept me hidden from the receptionist, long walks to the meeting room, and high tables with low chairs.

None of these barriers kept me out of a school, they just slowed me down as I walked farther from a parking place and waited for someone to help me up a step or ring the bell. Sometimes I risked using a bathroom without locking the door and other times I asked someone to stand outside to stop an unwanted intrusion into the bathroom I was using.

On return visits to many schools, I knew to bring my scooter. One time I made the wrong call in choosing a parking place. I parked on open grass next to the driveway close to the front door. Halfway through the IEP meeting, the assistant principal tracked me down and asked me to move my car from the bus loading zone. I returned to the meeting looking like a drowned rat after sloshing through the pouring rain without an umbrella.

When I hung up my hat at retirement, I was encouraged by the many appreciative comments I received from parents and professionals. Comments like the following confirmed that my education advocacy had made a difference:

- You gave [us] hope again.

- Your presence at my son's meetings gave me con-

fidence that the school would do what they're supposed to.

- You are a source of knowledge, inspiration and
  comfort.

- I always appreciated when you were in a meeting,
  looking out for our students and their rights in a
  friendly, logical, kind way.

- You always kept the student at the forefront of the
  discussion and the need to do what was right, not
  just by law but by common sense and humane action.

- You are a light in this world.

Naturally, I appreciated the feedback, but attribute my
reputation as a problem solver to Solomon's wisdom:

Patient persuasion can break down
the strongest resistance
and can even convince rulers.
~ Proverbs 25:15, GNT

Epilogue

After writing this book, I still have lingering questions. *How long before my advocacy is redundant? Will there be people to advocate for progress in nonprofits when negative forces run wild? Who will take up the mantle against dwarf tossing the next time it rears its ugly head? How long will it take before people with dwarfism and disabilities have equal access to public facilities and education?*

I recognize that advocacy has already done a lot to include people with dwarfism and other disabilities in the mainstream. And the advocacy toolkit has strengthened with the passing of each decade:

- 60 plus years as an LPA community

- 50 plus years as a member of a little people organization

- 40 plus years since adoption of the federal regulations implementing section 504 of the Rehabilitation Act

- 30 plus years since passage of the ADA

- 20 plus years since LPA submitted official comments to the federal Access Board in support of breaking the six-inch reach barrier

- 10 years since we beat back the attempt to repeal

Florida's law banning dwarf tossing in licensed establishments

Our collective voice has grown loud enough that federal laws now protect our civil rights; yet the need for disability advocacy has not dissipated. As long as there are people living on this planet, there will be a demand for disability advocates to implement these laws. It is our job to train up people to follow in our footsteps teaching them that change is possible with preparation, perseverance, persuasion, and prayer.

People with dwarfism and disabilities have a long way to go before we achieve an acceptable level of equal access and respect. Here are a few reminders of how much work remains to be done:

- Inaccessible service counters

- Heavy doors

- Staircases with useless or missing handrails

- Inaccessible medical equipment

- Inaccessible trains, taxis, and ride-share services

- Poor elevator maintenance or no elevator at all

- Otherwise accessible bathrooms made inaccessible with noncompliant installation of toilet paper, hand towels, or soap dispensers.

- And so much more . . .

I retired from paid employment as an advocate to complete this dwarfism trilogy, but as a colleague wrote, "Advocating for others never stops for people like us because it is where our heart is."

I agree. I've been an advocate for as long as I can remember and expect my advocacy will continue until the day I die or until Jesus returns, whichever comes first.

Acknowledgments

Editor: Vicki Prather, PratherInk Literary Services

Cover design: Michelle Stevens, www.mstevedesign.com

Cover Photographers: Cristina Tenney (front), Susan Sprayberry (back)

Front cover photo models: Michelle Stevens and Jeremy Pukahi

Back cover photo: Author, Angela Muir Van Etten

Typesetter: Roseanna M. White, roseannawhitedesigns.com

Endorsements: Gary Arnold, Genevieve Cousminer, Jim Kay, Dan Kennedy, and Bill Klein

Proofreaders: April Epperson, Carol Snyder, Deborah Coote, Greg Muir, and Diane Tomasik

Book launch team: Brenda Bell, Juliette Glasow, Susan Hansen, Donna Hosang, Ann Koebe, Pat Raybuck, Maria Telesca, and Mark Trombino

Website—angelamuirvanetten.com—Brenda Bell, BCP Data Services Inc.

Preview of Book II

PASS ME YOUR SHOES:
*A Couple with Dwarfism Navigates Life's Detours
with Love and Faith*

Chapter 1

My Heart Beat Faster

Washington Arrival

I jumped off the bottom step of the Dulles airport bus into a dimly lit Washington, DC, neighborhood. The 12- to 15-inch jump was required because my knees don't bend, and there was no handrail to aid my descent. I made a safe landing onto the sidewalk 8,500 miles from home, but I was exhausted—it was nearly midnight—and no one was there to greet me.

I wasn't surprised. Harriet Stickney had already told me she'd failed in her attempt to get the president of Little People of America (LPA) to meet me at the airport. As LPA's national correspondent, she viewed my position as president of Little People of New Zealand (LPNZ) worthy of a presidential welcome, not to mention extending the courtesy to a female in an unknown territory at night. After all, Harriet and her husband, Al, had shown me legendary hospitality in their San Francisco home for an entire week.

But there was no persuading President Bobby Van Etten. His January move to Arlington, Virginia, from the small town of Jupiter, Florida, hadn't prepared him for driving in DC, so he was more afraid of getting lost than any wrath coming his way from Harriet. Thankfully, a cab was available to transport me safely to my room at the International Guest House.

The guesthouse hosts were impressed that flowers preceded my arrival. When Bobby was unable to persuade Ernie—a friend and lifetime resident of the area—to meet me at the airport, the two greeted me with flowers instead. And a note from Bobby asking me to call him in the morning.

New Zealand Embassy Meeting

We met the next day at the NZ Embassy. The advantage was definitely mine, as Harriet had shared her opinion of the man and a few media articles written about him.

Bobby had moved from Florida in January 1981 for a job as a communications engineer for the Architectural and Transportation Barriers Compliance Board (Access Board). Unfortunately for Bobby, President Reagan made good on his 1980 campaign promise to shrink the federal government. As his first official act after his inauguration, Reagan ordered a hiring freeze retroactive to January 20, 1981. Bobby had already acted on the written job offer, moved from Florida, signed an apartment lease, and reported to work on January 26, 1981. He was among the 1,800 workers shocked to learn that his position was eliminated. The national media covered Bobby's story as a hardship case:

Little People's President Has Conservative Views Tested
Job Freeze by Reagan is Upheld
Left out in cold, he chips at ice on federal hiring[1]

Bobby's knowledge of me was limited to what Harriet

had told him—I was president of LPNZ and a lawyer on a Winston Churchill Fellowship. However, he didn't know that my fellowship brought me to the United States for three months to research disability civil rights laws and public relations programs designed to improve attitudes towards people with disabilities, and he didn't know that LPA was 1 of 40 disability organizations included in my research. His engineering (analytical) mind assumed that a little person with a government fellowship was probably middle-aged with a diagnosis of achondroplasia—the most common type of dwarfism. He imagined me on the plump side at about four feet tall.

On Saint Patrick's Day, 1981, Bobby discovered that his assumptions were all wrong. I was a petite 27-year-old with Larsen Syndrome,[2] a very rare type of dwarfism. When Bobby walked towards my desk in the NZ Embassy library, he was all smiles. For some inexplicable reason my heart beat faster as he got closer to me. I don't remember a thing he said. I was unnerved by the proximity of his brown eyes gazing directly into mine. We were eye-to-eye because we were the same exact height—and that connection rarely happens to a little person.

Our First Outing

The NZ Embassy was a convenient place for Bobby to meet me at the beginning of a planned day of sightseeing. Our first stop was the Lincoln Memorial. It didn't take me long to understand Bobby's concern about getting lost on his way to the airport. In broad daylight, he was quite flustered finding his way to the Memorial. And the more lost he got, the faster he drove. He even resorted to asking me for directions— someone who had been in DC for less than 24 hours and could not even see out the car window.

Bobby eventually found his way; we parked and made our way across the street. He then graciously extended his hand to help me up a curb. However, he didn't release my hand after both my feet were set on the sidewalk. Not ready for such a bold move, I let go of his hand. After all, this could hardly be called a date.

We chose the elevator as a good alternative to the 57 steps to President Lincoln's statue that towered above us at more than six times our height. As presidents of two disability organizations, we couldn't help but be inspired by the display of Lincoln's words from the Gettysburg address: *all men are created equal.* We both knew what it was like to be treated as second-class citizens and shared a life mission to achieve equality for little people and others with disabilities.

Pizza was our choice for the evening meal. Corned beef and cabbage never crossed our minds until a drunken Irishman saw the arrival of two little people as a sign of his good luck. We had forgotten about the holiday. He invited himself to our table to share Irish jokes, an intrusion we tolerated for a few minutes. I was relieved and impressed with Bobby's diplomacy as he took charge when the man asked us to join him at the Saint Patrick's Day parade. Bobby declined the offer and persuaded him to move along. Instead of going to the parade, Bobby returned me to my guesthouse where he was more interested in kissing me good night on the cheek than kissing any blarney stone.

To read more of *Pass Me Your Shoes*, go to my website at https://angelamuirvanetten.com to find retail links to Amazon, Barnes and Noble and Books a Million.

Endnotes

Chapter 2, President Robert: The Second Term

1 Marge Carlisle, Paul and Ellie Jones, Martha Undercoffer, Robert and Angela Van Etten.

2 In 1985 and 1986, I partnered with LPA Treasurer, Tim Deatherage, to prepare the IRS application for section 501(c)(3) tax-exempt status.

3 Mark and Betsy Trombino; Harry, Carol, and Brendan McDonald; Leonard, Lenette and Joelle Sawisch; and Dr. Charles I. Scott, Jr..

4 Some of Robert's Chicago relatives—Aunt Dolly, Joyce Vincent, Mary Kay and Carolyn Bieker—were also in the audience.

5 Rutgers Medical School in Piscataway, New Jersey (June 21-22, 1985).

6 Johns Hopkins Medical Institutions in Baltimore, Maryland (June 20-21, 1986).

7 Skeletal Dysplasia Symposium at the Henry Ford Hospital in Detroit, Michigan (July 19, 1986).

8 On October 28, 1986, the IRS granted interim approval for LPA's section 501(c)(3) tax-exempt status. Prior to the expiry of the Advance Ruling Period on December 31, 1989, I continued to work with LPA Treasurer, Tim Deatherage, to obtain final approval. At the same time, we successfully opposed the recommendation of an LPA Blue Ribbon Committee for the organization to reverse course and relinquish its 501(c)(3) status.

9 Harry and Carol McDonald founded the Short Stature library with medical and social articles on dwarfism. The LPA Foundation paid for a copy machine rental and almost 10,000 copies

distributed to chapters and districts at the St Louis conference in 1984.

10 "LPA's Medical Resource Center," LPA, accessed January 7, 2021, https://www.lpaonline.org/medical-resource-center.

11 Discussed in Chapter 9, Chicago Contest Planned.

12 Dwarf Athletic Association of America (DAAA), accessed January 7, 2021, http://www.daaa.org/history-of-daaa.html

Chapter 3, Vision to Reshape LPA

1 Robert coordinated Florida district meetings in Fort Myers (Spring 2001), Boca Raton (Fall 2001), St. Augustine (Spring 2002), Tampa (Fall 2002), Fort Lauderdale Beach (Spring 2003), and Gainesville (Fall 2003).

2 One workshop was "Employment Discrimination under the ADA"; the other was co-presented with Cara Egan, VP of PR, "Getting Your Elected Representatives to Work for You."

3 The railroad follows the farmlands of the Heber Valley and the shore of Deer Creek Reservoir, accessed November 25, 2020. https://www.hebervalleyrr.org/.

4 Ken and Patsy Swinson were close friends from our year living in Baltimore, Maryland. Their son, Kris, has the same type of dwarfism as Robert.

5 Kennedy, Dan. Little People: Learning to See the World Through My Daughter's Eyes. Rodale Books, 2003. https://www.amazon.com/books.

6 "Crosswalk Flags," Salt Lake City Transportation Division, accessed November 25, 2020, http://www.slcdocs.com/transportation/Pedestrian/pdf/CrosswalkFlagsBrochure11_05.pdf.

Chapter 4, Galvanize the Group and Heal the Breaches

1 I served the LPA Board of Directors as parliamentarian in 2002, 2003, and the first half of 2004.

Chapter 5, Destructive Forces and Direct Hits

1 The panel of LPA members included a retired judge, a licensed attorney, and a past president.

2 Two 19th-century feuding families from West Virginia and Kentucky.

3 An elderly church couple from a mobile home park, Veda and Dick, and Robert's cousins: Bill, Lyn, and Brett.

4 When we lose power, we also lose water since our well and pump are run by electricity. However, we purchased a hand pump for the well in preparation for the dire Y2K predictions.

5 In 2017 when sheltering from Hurricane Irma, Robert advanced to using a scooter battery to charge our cell phones, since we no longer had a boat.

6 Robert's elderly Aunt Rita and Uncle Bob brought their lounge chairs, cousins Gary and Kathryn catered to their needs, and Bill and Brett remembered the routine from two weeks earlier.

7 The damages caused by hurricanes Frances and Jeanne were eight and six billion dollars respectively, NOAA, accessed April 25, 2019, https://www.nhc.noaa.gov/pastcost.shtml. Where we live, the property appraiser assessed damages at $276 million with 23,000 homes impacted.

8 Turner, Jim. "Stuart Causeway reopens; residential damage in Martin reaches $50 million," TC Palm, part of the USA Today Network, October 28, 2005, https://www.tcpalm.com/tcp/local_news/article/0,2545,TCP_16736_4192007,00.html.

9 The Executive Committee members received a confidential print copy of the report via the US Postal Service.

Chapter 6, Presidential Relay Team

1 The designated duties of VP of Membership are too many to list, but included:

- Responding to hardship member applications and individual member queries on job discrimination, harassment, or other personal matters

- Coordinating incentive gifts to donors

- Showing members how one vote can make a difference to an election outcome

- Giving counsel to Executive Committee members on their duties

- Writing official conference invitation letters to support visa applications of international guests.

My undesignated duties included:

- Welcoming newly elected district and chapter officers

- Encouraging board members with personal Thanksgiving and New Year e-greetings

- Complimenting district directors for positive organizational initiatives, and sending expressions of caring and concern for officers experiencing sickness, surgeries, deaths in the family, and other difficulties.

2 Mary Grace Duffy of Cambridge Hill Partners, Inc., accessed, November 25, 2020, https://www.cambridgehill.com/.

3 The Strategic Plan was approved on April 3, 2005, with only one negative vote. There were ten goals that covered the national office location, leadership continuity, "brand identity," financial accountability, fundraising, communications, membership retention and recruitment, outreach, and adoption.

4 I contributed to 21 consecutive Monthly Messages published from November 2004 to June 2006.

5 In one of my first duties as LPA president, I chaired the December e-meeting to obtain board approval of the six-month contract the Executive Committee negotiated with Alyssa as LPA interim development director.

6 Natalie had significant database management experience and a Bachelor's degree in Computer Science. She oversaw prepara-

tion of the Database Procedures Manual and performed the first mail merge of the Membership Renewal Form exporting data directly from Raiser's Edge into Access. She also went to the LPA office to teach Samantha, the staff person, how to do this data export and continued to provide guidance from a distance.

7 See Appendix A.

Chapter 7, President Angela: Last Leg of Relay

1 The candidate had met the bylaw deadline when announcing to run for senior vice president, but after the deadline, wanted to transfer his candidacy to vice president of Membership.

2 I chaired three email meetings, four teleconference meetings, and the old business agenda of the annual meeting in Milwaukee, Wisconsin.

3 The Media award went to the Learning Channel for the many educational programs dedicated to dwarfism, such as: Dwarfs: Little People, Big Steps; Dwarf Family: Meet the Fooses; Incredibly Small: Kenadie's Story; Little People: Big Convention; Little People, Big Dreams; Little People: Big Lives; Little People, Big World; and The Smallest People in the World.

4 The Kitchens Meritorious Service Award went to Leonard Sawisch, PhD. Len had many roles in LPA, but is most beloved for his humor, musical talent as a drummer, disability activism, and founder of DAAA.

Chapter 8, First Reports

1 1985 Press Release of the ARRG, the English organization for short statured persons.

2 Irv Kupcinet, "Kup's Column," Chicago Sun Times (November 12, 1985).

3 Royko Column. "Great dwarf toss," Plain Dealer (Cleveland): "Will dwarf throwing catch on in our bars? Small chance," Pittsburgh Press; and in many other newspapers around the country (March 7, 1985).

4 ibid.

5 "Dwarf Tossing Contest Halted in Chicago," LPA Today, Vol. 23, No. 1 (Jan-Feb 1986).

6 1985 Press Release of the ARRG.

7 "The President's Golden Column," LPA Today, Jan-Feb 1986, Vol 23, No.1.

8 Craig McCulloh, letter to Mike Royko, Chicago Tribune, (March 21, 1985).

9 Steve Absalom, "Beware! Dwarfs are flying tonight," Stage and Television Today, (May 16, 1985).

10 Paul Hemp, "In Europe, Outcry Is Loud Over a Sport Called Dwarf Tossing." Wall Street Journal (November 1, 1985).

11 ibid.

12 BYKM: Belangevereniging voor kleine mensen.

13 Australia, Belgium, Canada, Costa Rica, Eire, France, Great Britain, India, Israel, Malaysia, New Zealand, Norway, South Africa, Sweden, Switzerland, the United States of America and West Germany. For specific information on any one of these organizations, write to the International Coordinator, Miss Pam Rutt, 24 Pinchfield, Maple Cross, Rickmansworth, Herts WD2 2TP, England.

14 Pam Rutt, Acting Chairperson of the ARRG, "Dwarfs 'denied any shred of human dignity': A degrading spectacle," letter to the editor, Stage and Television Today, (May 16, 1985).

15 Pam Rutt, letter to Robert and Angela Van Etten, (December 6, 1985).

Chapter 9, Chicago Contest Planned

1 Tom Fitzpatrick, "Bears dwarf pub's event," Chicago Sun Times (November 18, 1985).

2 "Great dwarf toss," Plain Dealer (Cleveland); "Will dwarf throwing catch on in our bars? Small chance," Pittsburgh Press; and in many other newspapers around the country (March 7, 1985).

3 Ibid.

4 Why dwarf tossing just won't fly," Delaware County Daily Times; "Dwarf tossing leaps to American shores" Orlando Sentinel Star; and in many other newspapers around the country (October 3, 1985).

5 Paul Hemp, "In Europe, Outcry Is Loud Over a Sport Called Dwarf Tossing," Wall Street Journal (November 1, 1985).

6 Kup's Column (November 2, 1985); the game between the Chicago Bears and the Dallas Cowboys was a crucial football game in the 1985 US Super Bowl series which the Chicago Bears went on to win.

7 See article reprinted in Appendix B.

8 Craig McCulloh, "Dwarf Tossing Contest Halted in Chicago," LPA Today, Vol 23, No. 1 (Jan-Feb 1986).

9 Jim Quinlan, "Dwarf toss event canceled here," Chicago Sun Times (November 18, 1985).

10 "So where do you go to get a dwarf tossing license?" Syracuse Herald Journal; "Dwarf tossing cut short," Pittsburgh Press; and in many other newspapers around the country (November 1985).

11 Jim Quinlan, Chicago Sun Times, (November 18, 1985).

12 Union Sun, Journal of Lockport New York (November 1985).

Chapter 10, Stop the Spread

1 "Dwarf Tossing Contest Halted in Chicago," LPA Today, Vol. 23, No. 1 (Jan-Feb 1986).

2 Pennsylvania Dutch Chapter newsletter of the LPA, Inc. (December 1985).

3 Harry McDonald, "The Power of Advocacy," newsletter of District 2 of the LPA, Inc. (January-April, 1986).

4 Ad in the personal column, Downtown: The Unbound Magazine, Rochester, New York (April 1, 1986).

5 Mary Anne Panarese, chapter president, Mohawk Valley Chapter newsletter (April, 1986).

6 The United Cerebral Palsy Association, the Disabled Veteran's

Organization, two members of the City Council, the State Attorney General's Office, and the Pennsylvania Liquor Control Board.

[7] Panarese, chapter newsletter (April, 1986).

[8] "Why dwarf tossing just won't fly," Delaware County Daily Times; "Dwarf tossing leaps to American shores" Orlando Sentinel Star; and in many other newspapers around the country (October 3, 1985).

[9] "So where do you go to get a dwarf tossing license?" Syracuse Herald Journal; "Dwarf tossing cut short," Pittsburgh Press; and in many other newspapers around the country (November 1985).

[10] "Why dwarf tossing just won't fly," Delaware County Daily Times; "Dwarf tossing leaps to American shores" Orlando Sentinel Star; and in many other newspapers around the country (October 3, 1985).

[11] Paul Hemp, "In Europe, Outcry Is Loud Over a Sport Called Dwarf Tossing," Wall Street Journal (November 1, 1985).

[12] ibid.

[13] ibid.

[14] ibid. According to later reports, one further contest took place in Brisbane, Australia on November 11, 1986. However, subsequent contests planned for Sydney and Melbourne in Australia, in the International Test Match series between England and Australia, were canceled in response to public protest, People Australia (December 22, 1986), and Times Union, Rochester, New York (November 13, 1986).

[15] "So where do you go to get a dwarf tossing license?," Syracuse Herald Journal; "Dwarf tossing cut short," Pittsburgh Press; and in many other newspapers around the country (November 1985).

[16] The argument was presented to a Florida court, in World Fair Freaks & Attractions, Inc. v Hodges (1972, Fla) 267 So 2d 817, 62 ALR 3d 1232, by the state in an attempt to prohibit the commercial exhibition of any crippled or physically distorted, mal-

formed or disfigured person in any place where admission fees were charged. In this case, one of the persons being exhibited was a dwarf. However, the court did not uphold the state's interest in preventing such exhibitions; rather it declared the statute as unconstitutional because of the failure to provide reasonable standards to be followed in the statute's application.

17 This view was expressed at a chapter meeting by the members of the Mid-Hudson Valley Chapter of the LPA, Inc. (November 16, 1985).

Chapter 11, Biting the Legislative Dust

1 Heidi and John Heinrich, Barbara Jones, Jim and Beth Tatman, and John and Nancy Mayeux, were the lead LPA advocates against dwarf tossing in Florida.

2 Show #502-9; Transcript #172. Other guests included Heidi Heinrich, Florida State Representative Michael Friedman, the road manager and owner of the dwarf tossing business, and two of the dwarfs paid to be tossed.

3 Florida Statutes, Title XXXIV, Alcoholic Beverages and Tobacco, Chapter 561, Beverage Law: Administration § 561.665 prohibits commercial establishments with a liquor license from undertaking or permitting any contest or promotion or other form of recreational activity involving exploitation endangering the health, safety, and welfare of any person with dwarfism. A violation of the law could result in suspension or revocation of the license, a civil penalty not to exceed $1,000, or both. The Florida Legislature, accessed November 25, 2020, http://www.leg.state.fl.us/STATUTES/index.cfm?App_mode=Display_Statute&Search_String=&URL=0500-0599/0561/Sections/0561.665.html.

4 Active members included Betty Adelson, Sy Agoss, Tom Aquafredda, Max Baumback, Mrs. Alfred Dyer, Jean Fairburn, Pat Henneman, Lori Kelly, Rachel Kleiman, Doreen Lackner, Al and Janet Pickard, Bill Roberts, Ann and Eugene Smith, Susan and Steven Smith, Frank and Gerri Taddeo, Eileen Teachout, and Patricia Yoder.

5 The Florida legislative package included: "LPA's Position Paper on Dwarf Tossing," talking points on "Why Dwarf Tossing Should Be Illegal;" and "Sample Responses to Objections to the Bill."

6 Drive Time with Perry Stone and Laurie Thompson.

7 What We'll Do for Entertainment." Show #1012-9; Transcript #101289.

8 Assemblyman Michael Bragman (D-North Syracuse) and William Larkin, Jr. (R-New Windsor) sponsored Assembly bill (A. 8919) and Senator Nicholas Spano (R-Yonkers) sponsored the Senate bill (S. 6559). Mary Beth Primo of Assemblyman Bragman's office was an invaluable resource in guiding me through the legislative process.

9 Kyle Smith, "Labor Sec is a living doll, says big Bill." New York Post, October 20, 1993.

10 A second Senate vote was needed to approve the revised language in the Assembly version of the bill.

11 "No retail licensee for on-premises consumption shall suffer or permit any contest or promotion which endangers the health, safety, and welfare of any person with dwarfism. Any retail licensee in violation of this section shall be subject to the suspension or revocation of said licensee's license to sell alcoholic beverages for on-premises consumption. For the purposes of this section, the term "dwarfism" means a condition of being abnormally small which is caused by heredity, endocrine dysfunction, renal insufficiency or deficiency or skeletal diseases that result in disproportionate short stature and adult height of less than four feet ten inches." New York Law, Alcoholic Beverage Control, Article 8, § 106(6-b). FindLaw, accessed December 15, 2020. https://codes.findlaw.com/ny/alcoholic-beverage-control-law/abc-sect-106.html.

12 Newman, Peter. "The worst of 1990: vintage year for greed." Maclean Hunter Limited, December 24, 1990, accessed December 15, 2020, https://macleansarchive.azurewebsites.net/article/1990/12/24/the-worst-of-1990-vintage-year-for-greed.

Chapter 12, Give Me A Break

1 San Francisco Bay Guardian Online, December 29, 1999. http://www.sfbayguardian.com/News/34/13/ofinvent.html.

2 Robert and I were both interviewed by John Stossel of 20/20, a Canadian network, and ABC of Australia. I was also interviewed by Sat 1 (a German satellite network with CBS news feeds), and the Palm Beach Post. Fox News interviewed Robert. Nancy Mayeux and I were interviewed on the Sally Jessy Raphael Show, broadcast on April 18, 2002.

3 As a volunteer organization, LPA had no paid staff assigned to monitor agency notices of proposed rulemaking.

4 See articles on John Stossel at Fairness and Accuracy in Reporting (FAIR), a national media watch group offering well-documented criticism of Stossel's media bias and censorship. Fairness and Accuracy in Reporting, accessed April 25, 2019, https://www.fair.org/.

5 Van Etten, C. Angela. "John Stossel Compromises Dwarfs in Name of Freedom." March 2002. The article was posted on an LPA dwarfism listserv, the LPA website, and is reprinted in Appendix C.

6 Rule Title: Exploitation of Dwarfs, 61A-3.048. Florida Administrative Code, accessed November 25, 2020, https://www.fl-rules.org/gateway/ruleno.asp?id=61A-3.048.

7 Florida Statute, Title XXXIV, Alcoholic Beverages and Tobacco §§ 561.29, 561.665. The Florida Legislature, accessed November 25, 2020, http://www.leg.state.fl.us/STATUTES/index.cfm?App_mode=Display_Statute&Search_String=&URL=0500-0599/0561/Sections/0561.665.html.

Chapter 13, A Perennial Weed

1 Rohrlich, Justin. "Florida Rep. Has Plan to Revitalize Dwarf Tossing Industry." Signs of the Times, October 7, 2011, accessed November 25, 2020, https://www.sott.net/article/235987-Florida-Rep-Has-Plan-to-Revitalize-Dwarf-Tossing-Industry.

2 Augustine, Matt. "FL Representative Wants to Repeal Ban on Dwarf Tossing." 104.5 WOKV, October 20, 2011. http://www.wokv.com/news/news/local/fl-representative-wants-re-peal-ban-dwarf-tossing/nFKcJ/; Michael McLaughlin. "Ritch Workman, Florida Lawmaker, Says Yes To 'Dwarf-Toss-ing,' No To Gay Marriage." http://www.huffingtonpost.com/2011/10/25/ritch-workman-dwarf-tossing_n_1025112.html

3 ibid.

4 "Repeal 'dwarf tossing' ban, Workman urges. Big government hurts little people, legislator insists." Florida Today, October 8, 2011. http://www.floridatoday.com/article/20111008/NEWS01/310080019/Repeal-dwarf-tossing-ban-Work-man-urges?odyssey=nav%7Chead; James Garton. "The cure for unemployment: Legalized dwarf tossing." Philadelphia Finance Examiner (October 29, 2011). http://www.examiner.com/finance-in-philadelphia/the-cure-for-unemployment-le-galized-dwarf-tossing.

5 "LPA Dwarfism Awareness Month Press Release." LPA, September 13, 2011. https://www.lpaonline.org/index.php?op-tion=com_content&view=article&id=68&tmpl=component.

6 LPA resistance team members included: President Gary Arnold; Executive Director Joanna Campbell; VP of PR Leah Smith; Membership Director Ethan Crough; Advocacy Director Joe Stramondo; past presidents Robert Van Etten and Angela Van Etten; District 4 Director David Doidge; and LPA advocates Steven Cotoia and Clinton Brown.

7 Email to Angela Van Etten from Joe Stramondo on October 9, 2011.

8 "Statement of LPA regarding proposed legislation that repeals a ban on dwarf tossing." LPA, October 12, 2011. http://www.lpaonline.org/mc/page.do?sitePageId=129787&orgId=lpa.

9 The Spanish Inquisition, advertising, and nuclear war. December 29, 1999. San Francisco Bay Guardian Online, March 8, 2002. http://www.sfbayguardian.com/News/34/13/ofinvent.html.

[10] Politics. "Ritch Workman, Florida State Representative, Proposes Repeal Of 'Dwarf Tossing' Ban." HuffPost, October 6, 2011, accessed November 25, 2020, https://www.huffpost.com/entry/ritch-workman-florida-dwarf-tossing-law_n_998155.

[11] McLaughlin, Michael. HuffPost, January 13, 2012, updated February 21, 2012, accessed November 26, 2020, http://www.huffingtonpost.com/2012/01/13/dwarf-paralyzed-after-bar-tossing_n_1204799.html?ref=weird-news.

[12] Moye, David. "Florida Dwarf Tossing Ban Repeal Dropped by Bill Sponsor Ritch Workman." HuffPost, April 12, 2012, accessed November 26, 2020, https://www.huffingtonpost.com/2012/04/12/florida-dwarf-tossing-ban-repeal-ritch-workman_n_1421037.html.

[13] Klein, Bill. "Dwarf Tossing Should Be Illegal." Daily Beast, Oct 23, 2011 10:00 AM EDT. http://www.thedailybeast.com/articles/2011/10/23/dwarf-tossing-should-be-illegal-says-reality-show-star.html.

[14] Ibid.

[15] Afghanistan, Antigua and Barbuda, Australia, Brazil, Canada, Chile, France, Germany, Ireland, Israel, Italy, Japan, Korea, Netherlands Republic, New Zealand, Norway, Pakistan, Peru, Philippines, Portugal, Saudi Arabia, Sweden, Switzerland, Taiwan, United Kingdom, United States, US minor outlying islands, and Uruguay.

[16] Joint letter to Rep. Workman from Gary Arnold, LPA president and Mark Perriello, president of the American Association of People with Disabilities (November 14, 2011).

[17] ibid.

[18] In 2010, I was appointed by the governor of Florida to serve a three-year term on the Florida Independent Living Council (FILC), tasked, among other things, with writing the three-year state plan for independent living for the 15 or so centers for independent living in Florida. Florida Independent Living Council, accessed December 16, 2020, http://www.floridasilc.org/.

[19] The folder included the FILC advocacy platform, the LPA posi-

tion statement, LPA's letter to Workman, my Huffington Post blog entry, and the Florida Disability Rights letter.

20 Last Action: March 9, 2012, House - Died in Business and Consumer Affairs Subcommittee. Florida Senate, accessed November 26, 2020, https://www.flsenate.gov/Session/Bill/2012/4063.

Chapter 14, Let Me Ride

1 "Saul Alinsky." Conservapedia, accessed November 25, 2020. http://conservapedia.com/Saul_Alinsky.

2 ibid.

3 Alinsky, Saul. "Rules for Radicals." 1971. Conservapedia, accessed November 26, 2020. https://www.conservapedia.com/Rules_for_Radicals; Atkinson, Jay. "Saul Alinsky." The Latter Rain, accessed November 26, 2020. latter-rain.com/ltrain/alinski.htm.

4 Ibid.

5 Ibid.

6 First published by Lawyers Cooperative Publishing in 1992 with continuing updates by Thomson Reuters.

Chapter 15, Breaking the Six-Inch Reach Barrier

1 The ANSI Access Code becomes enforceable law when adopted by state and local governments. Many of its provisions also form the basis for the federal access code known as the ADAAG which becomes enforceable law when adopted by federal government agencies.

2 The International Code Council/American National Standards Institute (ICC/ANSI) A117.1 Committee on Accessible and Usable Buildings and Facilities has the following categories of membership:

- Consumer/users requiring accessibility
- Professional organizations involved in research, testing, consulting, education, engineering, or design

- Builder/owner/operators involved in development, construction, ownership, and operation of buildings and facilities
- Producer/distributors of manufactured products
- Regulatory agencies or organizations that promulgate or enforce codes or standards.

3 The Measure-Up Campaign results were documented in multiple tables and graphs in a study called the "Anthropometric National Survey of Adult Dwarfs." Robert Van Etten compiled the data and Dr. Steinfeld confirmed its accuracy. The reliability of the data was corroborated by the "Functional Health Survey" of Dr. Michael Goldberg and the "Anthropometric Measures and Sports Performance of Dwarf Athletes Survey" of Dr. Leslie Low.

4 American Council for the Blind, American Foundation for the Blind, the Disability Rights Education and Defense Fund, National Association of the Deaf, President's Committee of Employment of People with Disabilities, Paralyzed Veterans of America, Self Help for Hard of Hearing People, United Cerebral Palsy Association, and World Institute on Disability.

5 A side reach means that a user is able to access equipment (not just a gas pump) by coming alongside the device. This is especially significant for wheelchair users where insufficient turning space makes a side reach impossible. When this happens, the reach is obstructed by the wheelchair forced to face the device in a forward position in which case the user must reach across their lap and wheelchair footrests. When a forward reach is necessary, the reach is called obstructed and the device must be lowered in accordance with the applicable building code.

6 The elevator industry was put on notice that LPA would propose removal of this exception in the next revision cycle. On June 4, 1996, the National Elevator Industry Institute (NEII) met with Robert and I in Rochester, New York to understand the access needs of little people and to explore ways of providing 100% elevator access in the future.

7 More than a half million people whose disability involved a

reach limitation—including some wheelchair users and people with cerebral palsy—would also benefit from breaking the six-inch reach barrier. Source: 56 FR 35408, 35430 (July 26, 1991); 57 FR 19472 (May 6, 1992); 57 FR 41006 (September 8, 1992).

8 "Obstructed Reach Range Survey of Adult Dwarfs." LPA, August 1996.

9 The ICC/ANSI A117.1 Standard for Accessible and Usable Buildings and Facilities is updated on a five-year cycle.

Chapter 16, Battle for Access in Different Forums

1 In June 1999, I was unanimously elected as the vice chair of the ICC/ANSI Access Committee. I only took this position because it gave LPA a voice in policy decisions at the Executive Committee level and because the chairperson was very healthy. My purpose for being at the meetings was to advocate, not moderate meetings. I continued in this position until February 2002 when I stepped down as the LPA delegate.

2 LPA Access Committee members were Jonathan North, Paul Olson, and Chris Figone.

3 Testimony was given by David Brookfield, Cara Egan, Colleen Gioffreda, Dan Okenfuss, and Michelle Parisi.

4 Cara Egan, Dan Okenfuss, and Francine and Lydia Barber.

5 "ADA and ABA Accessibility Guidelines." United States Access Board, July 23, 2004, https://www.access-board.gov/guide-lines-and-standards/buildings-and-sites/about-the-ada-stan-dards/background/ada-aba-accessibility-guidelines-2004. The 2004 ADAAG was effective on September 21, 2004. No such exception is provided in the ANSI Access standard.

6 Jeff Lewis, Chris O'Neill, Robert, and myself.

7 § 407.4.6.1, [Elevator Car Controls] Location. Exception 1, ICC/ANSI A117.1-2003.

8 The LPA/NEII proposal was accepted at the May 2002 ANSI Access Committee meeting and appears in § 407.4.8, ICC/ANSI A117.1-2003.

9 "Obstructed Reach Range Survey of Adult Dwarfs." LPA, August 1996.

10 § 606.5. Lavatories and Enhanced Reach Range. ICC/ANSI A117.1-2003.

Chapter 17, Advocate for Independent Living

1 "History of Independent Living," Center for Independent Living of North Central Florida, accessed January 1, 2021. http://cilncf.org/cil-history/.

2 The federal Medicaid Waiver programs allow states to provide Medicaid services to consumers in their homes and communities and waive the eligibility requirement that a person must live in an institution.

3 The American Red Cross of Martin County, the ARC of Martin County, the City of Stuart, Deaf and Hard of Hearing Services of the Treasure Coast, Helping People Succeed, the ADA Coordinator for Martin County, Martin County Emergency Management, and Martin Memorial Health Systems.

4 The ErgoChair for Little People is sold by Assisting Little People, accessed April 21, 2021, https://www.assistinglittlepeople.com/ergochair-for-little-people.html.

Chapter 18, Transit Funding and Public Participation

1 Daphne Duret, "Elderly and disabled ask Martin commission not to cut buses." Palm Beach Post (June 17, 2008); George Andreassi, "Disabled fight for Stuart public transit." Stuart News (June 17, 2008); R.J. Harrington, "Community Coach riders protest to keep a slice of Martin budget." Stuart News (June 18, 2008).

2 This increase was partly due to a 2008 federal law that increased to 50% the amount of federal transit dollars local governments could spend on operating costs.

3 The Alzheimer's Association, ARC of Martin County, Braille International, Coalition for Independent Living Options, Division of Blind Services, and Division of Vocational Rehabilitation.

4 The Florida Commission for the Transportation Disadvantaged (CTD), accessed December 21, 2020. https://ctd.fdot.gov/index.htm. In Martin County, the program is administered by the Martin Metropolitan Planning Organization (MPO), the Martin Board of County Commissioners (BOCC), the Martin Transportation Disadvantaged Local Coordinating Board, and the Community Transportation Coordinator (CTC).

Chapter 19, Social Security Benefits Representation

1 In 2008, substantial gainful activity (SGA) for individuals with disabilities who are not blind was $940 a month; in 2021, SGA is $1,310. A higher SGA rate is applied to people who are blind. Social Security Administration, accessed December 26, 2020. https://www.ssa.gov/oact/cola/sga.html.

2 See section 301 of the Social Security Disability Amendments of 1980, P.L. 96-265 and its implementing regulations at 20 CFR §§404.327, 404.328, and 416.1338.

Chapter 20, Special Education for Students with Disabilities

1 "Thirty-five Years of Progress in Educating Children With Disabilities Through IDEA." Office of Special Education and Rehabilitative Services. US Department of Education, accessed January 2, 2021. https://www2.ed.gov/about/offices/list/osers/idea35/history/index_pg10.html

2 "The Condition of Education: Students with Disabilities." National Center for Education Statistics, updated May 2020, accessed January 2, 2021. https://nces.ed.gov/programs/coe/indicator_cgg.asp

3 The Education for All Handicapped Children Act of 1975, PL 94-142, 20 U.S.C. §§1400-1461.

4 "A History of the Individuals with Disabilities Education Act," US Department of Education, accessed January 2, 2021. https://sites.ed.gov/idea/IDEA-History

5 The ESE team leader or intervention problem-solving coach,

teachers, administrators, therapists, program specialists, behavior analysts, counselors, school nurses, and psychologists.

6 "I'll Make the Difference." Words and Music by Moses Hogan. Written for the American Cancer Society's Relay for Life.

Preview of Book II, Chapter 1 My Heart Beat Faster

1 Associated Press, Christopher Connell, "Little People's President Has Conservative Views Tested," February 5, 1981. Laura Kierman, "Job Freeze by Reagan is Upheld," Washington Post, (February 26, 1981). John Hicks, "Left out in cold, he chips at ice on federal hiring," Sentinel Star, (Orlando, FL), March 1, 1981.

2 "Larsen Syndrome," LPA Medical Resource Center, Dwarfism Types and Diagnoses, accessed April 22, 2019, https://www.lpaonline.org/medical-resource-center.

About the Author

As a dwarf of three-feet-four-inches, Angela has lived the disability experience and—for as long as she can remember—has advocated for herself and others as equal contributing members of society.

As a dual citizen of New Zealand and the United States, Angela qualified as a lawyer in both countries with admission to the bar in New Zealand, Ohio, and New York. As a lawyer in New Zealand, she advocated for clients in both civil and criminal courts.

LPA has twice awarded Angela its highest honor—the Kitchens Meritorious Service Award—for her work as a leader in banning dwarf tossing in licensed establishments in New York and Florida and in breaking the six-inch reach barrier in buildings and facilities open to the public throughout America. She has served as national president of LP organizations in both New Zealand and the United States.

Angela has media and public speaking experience in local, regional, national, and international markets and has been interviewed by TV icons such as Phil Donahue and Sally Jessy Raphael.

Angela has been a legal writer and editor of disability civil rights law books for Thomson Reuters and a staff writer for the Christian Law Association. Her articles on dwarfism and disability advocacy have been published in *LPA Today*, and online in the *HuffPost* blog. Although this is the final book in Angela's dwarfism trilogy, her weekly blog posts will continue at https://angelamuirvanetten.com/blog.

Angela lives in Florida with her husband of 40 years where she is active in church ministry.

Stay Connected with the Author

Visit my website—https://angelamuirvanetten.com—a voice for people with dwarfism and disability, guided by faith and justice.

Subscribe to my (1) weekly blog and write a comment sharing your opinion, and (2) quarterly newsletter, go to https://angelamuirvanetten.com.

Email me at angela@angelamuirvanetten.com

FOLLOW ANGELA MUIR VAN ETTEN AT:

AMAZON AUTHOR CENTRAL
http://bit.ly/Angela-Muir-Van-Etten

FACEBOOK AUTHOR PAGE
https://www.facebook.com/MuirVanEttenTrilogy

INSTAGRAM
Angela Muir Van Etten

Twitter
https://twitter.com/muirvanetten

PINTEREST
https://www.pinterest.com/AngelaMuirVanEtten/

GOODREADS
https://www.goodreads.com/author/show/1705018.
Angela_Muir_Van_Etten